TRICKBOX OF MEMORY

BEFORE YOU START TO READ THIS BOOK, take this
moment to think about making a donation to
punctum books, an independent non-profit press,

@ https://punctumbooks.com/support/

If you're reading the e-book, you can click on the
image below to go directly to our donations site.
Any amount, no matter the size, is appreciated and
will help us to keep our ship of fools afloat. Contributions from dedicated readers will also help us to
keep our commons open and to cultivate new work
that can't find a welcoming port elsewhere. Our adventure is not possible without your support.

Vive la Open Access.

Fig. 1. Hieronymus Bosch, *Ship of Fools* (1490–1500)

First published in 2020 by punctum books, Earth, Milky Way.
https://punctumbooks.com

ISBN-13: 978-1-953035-24-0 (print)
ISBN-13: 978-1-953035-25-7 (ePDF)

DOI: 10.21983/P3.0298.1.00

LCCN: 2020950613
Library of Congress Cataloging Data is available from the Library of Congress

Copy Editing: Lily Brewer
Book Design: Vincent W.J. van Gerven Oei

punctumbooks

spontaneous acts of scholarly combustion

HIC SVNT MONSTRA

TRICKBOX OF MEMORY

Essays on Power and Disorderly Pasts

Felicitas Macgilchrist & Rosalie Metro (eds.)

p.

Contents

Reaching into the Trickbox of Memory

Rosalie Metro & Felicitas Macgilchrist

In 2009, John Sutton asked readers to "look beyond memory studies," in order to see how memory is used in different disciplines. In 2017, he observed how that has and has not happened over the past decade.[1] As he points out, the fact that "memory is so often in use when it is not explicitly in question remains a practical and intellectual challenge for movements towards integration, institutionalization, and discipline-formation in memory studies."[2] In other words, memory is everywhere we look, but hard to pin down, hard to "discipline." But memory cannot be captured in the ubiquitous image of a "black box" of entirely unknown processes. Memory is "entwined" with "cognitive and affective, bodily and social, technological and ecological" domains;[3] it cannot be easily separated from its contexts. As Sutton puts it, "phenomena of memory do not stay compartmentalised": we are not dealing with neatly-packed storage boxes arranged on a shelf.[4] These phenomena "circulate, they crop up

---

1   John Sutton, "Beyond Memory Again: Risk, Teamwork, Vicarious Remembering," *Memory Studies* 10, no. 4 (2017): 379.

2   Ibid.

3   Ibid.

4   Ibid., 382.

elsewhere, they fuel other personal, collaborative, and collective practices, in daily life, in the arts, in politics: memory repeatedly takes us beyond memory studies."[5] However, Sutton is optimistic that interdisciplinary teams of researchers can work together on memory, even if their collaborations are "fragile."[6]

Trickbox of Memory represents one such fragile collaboration. This trickbox — a box full of reflections on damaged, disorderly pasts and their repair — is adamantly not a black box nor a storage box nor a toolbox. It contains chapters written by scholars in different disciplines, by practitioners, theorists, and activists. It was assembled from the overflow of a symposium on memory practices, the "doing" of memory. We invited our favorite writers on memory to the symposium. Their thinking at the margins of established memory studies draws from literary criticism, post-qualitative inquiry, new materialism, and political activism. The conversations at the symposium were unexpected, urgent, and generative. Given the authors' disparate starting points, the book you now hold has been curated rather than controlled, the process of its assemblage anarchic rather than totalizing. We arrived at the metaphor of the "trickbox" because, while memory plays tricks on us, people also play tricks on each other and on themselves: sleights of hand in which one object is switched out for a nearly identical twin. Stories are respliced with whatever is up one's sleeve. Nations are sawed in half and then made to stand up and walk again.

The snippets below offer glimpses into the worlds you will pull out of this trickbox. Shake it up, then reach in and see what you find: maybe a tiny spaceship, maybe a signpost, a parade, a raised fist, an entire museum. This jumble of stuff may spark memories, prompt anticipation, or generate friction. You may try to make the parts mean something, or you may throw them back in and try your luck again. Concepts rub up against each other, pieces chip off, things leak, glitter gets everywhere. Some things are damaged, their edges are ragged. Others are half-way

---

5   Ibid.
6   Ibid., 380.

fixed. Yet others show the potential for repair in the future. This volume is a container, but it cannot contain what you do with its contents.

1. RUINS. (Heidi Grunebaum) Start with the ruins and the remapping of contested spaces. A simple journey to and through Lubya that is not so simple, people re-inscribing memory on Palestinian/Israeli land that is physically littered with the past, littered with inanimate and human obstacles.

2. MATERIALITY. (Alexandra Binnenkade & Felicitas Macgilchrist) What happens when we stop and pick up one object — for instance, the Friendship 7 spaceship with John Glenn inside? What happens when we put it in a museum, when we let the museum grow online?

3. INNOCENCE. (Lisa Farley) When we stop and pick up one object on our journey through the ruins, we risk erasing the idea of innocence, of innocent bystanders, of children and childhood itself. Who is allowed to have a childhood, and whose childhood is a casualty of history? The idea of innocence is a form of resistance to memories we do not want: the genocide of Indigenous Peoples and their ongoing marginalization.

4. RESPONSIBILITY. (Matthew Howard) Because we are not innocent, we have a responsibility to remember hitherto obscured pasts. Where are the experiences of Aboriginal and Torres Strait Islander people within the memory of Anzac? How has one account been sustained as a particular "truth" of Anzac Day? Who takes up this responsibility to remember in the present?

5. BODIES. (Rosalie Metro) The body takes up the responsibility to remember. Race is embodied memory, re-enacted against backdrops that are chillingly familiar and alarmingly new. The protests of Black students in Missouri is a counter-mem-

ory to the innocent past nostalgically constructed by white Americans.

6. HISTORY. (Alexandra Oeser) Maybe it is the idea of memory itself that keeps us tied to the nation. We want to look at the construction of the nation, but we keep turning to this more "innocent" notion of "memory" and "identity," hoping to escape politicization. But our little memories are not innocent, are not beside history but inside it.

7. QUESTIONS. (Elizabeth Anderson Worden) How do we as researchers construct memories through the questions we ask? The object is not just "there," to be studied. How are we constructing the discipline, and in the process, constructing nations or transnationalism, damage or repair?

As we lay these chapters side by side, we see that burrowing into them leaves you with a pile of rubble. Excavate this rubble and see what you find. Is the innocence central to Farley's idea of childhood embodied in the blond child who watches Black students in Missouri disrupt a parade with their own version of history? Is the responsibility that Howard advocates the one taken up through the re-occupation of the Palestinian village of Lubya? Is this procession through the ruins of Lubya a re-instantiation of the nation, as Oeser might fear? Are we even talking about the same things?

The strength and weakness of memory studies is its fragmentary nature, as Segesten and Wüstenberg point out in their piece exploring the state of this "emergent field."[7] In dragging together, naming, and boxing up these fragments (what else is editing a volume like this one?), we participate in the institutionalization that they say is essential to the future of memory studies. By choosing single words as chapter titles, we point to something in each which goes beyond memory. These words simultaneously

---

7   Anamaria Dutceac Segesten and Jenny Wüstenberg, "Memory Studies: The State of an Emergent Field," *Memory Studies* 10, no. 4 (June 2017): 474.

dismember memory studies by attending to "memory's specific activities and forms," and reanimate "memory" as a container for all of them.[8] In other words, we are performing memory studies in this book, helping to give it a past and a future, even as we position ourselves offstage, in its liminal spaces.

This performance is spontaneous but not haphazard. One core issue crystallizes across the chapters of this volume. With an orientation to social rather than political memory, an over-arching focus is the subtlety of how power relations are enacted and contested (economically, bodily, geographically, militarily, verbally) through references to the past. In each chapter, for instance, the trauma of racialization is somehow layered, welcome or unwelcome, into memory practices. In some contributions, this is made explicit (Metro, Binnenkade and Macgilchrist, Howard), in others, it is oblique. In each chapter, the sociality involved in producing "the past" is interlaced throughout the analysis, whether this is through public ceremony (Grunebaum) and protest (Metro), adults enacting their desire to protect children imagined as innocent (Farley), or the power-laden interactions between interviewer and interviewee (Worden). In each chapter, dominant attempts to shape traditional national identifications through memory are diffracted into the shaping of solidarities or other, reparative forms of community. This theme is, again, discussed more explicitly in some chapters (Grunebaum, Howard, Oeser) than in others. This collective attention to power relations across multiple dimensions of memory teaches us, perhaps, new tricks for engaging the critical potential of working with memory.

Whatever we learn, we learn it in what Walter Benjamin called a "moment of danger," when fascism threatens to rise again. As Levi and Rothberg point out, the phenomena of our time — "Trump and Brexit, Jobbik and Golden Dawn, Putin, Erdoğan, Modi, Le Pen, and el-Sisi" — invoke a nostalgic and

---

8   Susannah Radstone, "Reconceiving Binaries: The Limits of Memory," *History Workshop Journal* 59, no. 1 (Spring 2005): 134.

triumphant past, and threaten to revive it before our eyes.[9] As Levi and Rothberg note, "the memory of extreme forms of nationalism, racism, and reaction is not only the property of its victims, who have been central to much of the globalized memory discourse of the last decades; rather, nationalist, racist, and reactionary memories also help transmit the traditions of nativism, populism, and fascism that are referenced in far-right movements today."[10] In other words, "we" — the authors and readers of this volume — are not the only ones who remember and counter-remember. We are not alone in discovering this trickbox, nor in opening our eyes wide (but are they open in horror or in delight?) at discovering particular damaged pasts and attempts at reparation. What we construct as a moment of danger, others see as an opportunity to finally revive a lost paradise, to finally feel secure about the prospect of a better future.

This not-aloneness simultaneously creates the possibilities for transnational fantasies of purism and disperses attempts to disrupt these fantasies. "Orderly pasts" are the easiest to instrumentalize in the service of fascism. If anything unites the contributions in this volume, it is a commitment to throwing memory and history into disarray. Memory is always already "unfinished business."[11] That is why we offer you these disorderly pasts, reader, without an apology.

Acknowledgments

The symposium which brought the contributors of this volume into conversation was hosted at the Georg-Eckert-Institute for International Textbook Research (GEI) in Braunschweig, Germany and funded by the Leibniz Association through two research groups, *Memory Practices* and *Teaching the Cold War.*

---

9   Neil Levi and Michael Rothberg, "Memory Studies in a Moment of Danger: Fascism, Postfascism, and the Contemporary Political Imagination," *Memory Studies* 11, no. 3 (July 2018): 355–67.

10 Ibid., 356.

11 Benjamin Nienass and Ross Poole, "The Limits of Memory," *International Social Science Journal* 62, nos. 203–4 (March–June 2011): 89–102.

The volume was generously supported by the Leibniz Association's Open Access Monograph Publishing Fund. We thank Roman Richtera for his work developing this book project and our fellow symposium organizers, Barbara Christophe, Katharina Baier, Johanna Ahlrichs, and Patrick Mielke, for setting the conversations rolling. We have loved working with an amazing group of scholars on this volume, and thank the contributors for their creativity, their revisions, and their patience. Paul Schabacker deserves special thanks for his editorial assistance on the whole manuscript. We thank the editors and team at punctum books. Vincent W.J. van Gerven Oei, Eileen A. Fradenburg Joy, and Lily Brewer have been wonderful to work with. It is a privilege to be included in this truly open press that celebrates writing-as-opening. And Felicitas especially thanks Rosalie for joining as co-editor to help fill the trickbox and move the project to completion.

Bibliography

Levi, Neil, and Michael Rothberg. "Memory Studies in a Moment of Danger: Fascism, Postfacism, and the Contemporary Political Imagination." *Memory Studies* 11, no. 3 (July 2018): 355–67. DOI: 10.1177/1750698018771868.

Nienass, Benjamin, and Ross Poole. "The Limits of Memory." *International Social Science Journal* 62, nos. 203–4 (March–June 2011): 89–102. DOI: 10.1111/j.1468-2451.2011.01796.x.

Radstone, Susannah. "Reconceiving Binaries: The Limits of Memory." *History Workshop Journal* 59, no. 1 (Spring 2005): 134–50. DOI: 10.1093/hwj/dbi012.

Segesten, Anamaria Dutceac, and Jenny Wüstenberg. "Memory Studies: The State of the Field." *Memory Studies* 10, no. 4 (June 2017): 474–89. DOI: 10.1177/1750698016655394.

Sutton, John. "Beyond Memory Again: Risk, Teamwork, Vicarious Remembering." *Memory Studies* 10, no. 4 (2017): 379–83. DOI: 10.1177/1750698017725622.

1

Ruins

Heidi Grunebaum

A warm and windless spring afternoon in the Galilee. Being a
Friday, traffic on the main, arterial roads thins out as Jewish–
Israeli families rush home to prepare to welcome the Sabbath
at sunset. Accompanied by my daughter, I am staying with a
group of mainly Jewish South Africans in a hotel in Nazareth,
a hostel of sorts, for Christian pilgrims. We are with three Palestinian families, who, having been made refugees from their
ancestral village Lubya in July 1948, live in various Scandinavian
countries, part of a large Palestinian diaspora. We are close to
the village of Kufr Qana where Jesus is said to have made wine
from water. The hotel is near the top of a steep hill from Nazareth's main drag where I go to smoke shisha and search for cold
beer. That Friday afternoon, we are all in a mammoth tourist
bus — the three Palestinian families, my daughter and me, and
the mostly Jewish South African group — heaving its way down
the steep hill to take us to the Jewish National Fund's South Africa Forest.

The bus turns off the main road near the Golani junction,
previously the Maskanah junction, joining Nazareth to Tiberias
and drives into the parking area of the forest and leisure park.
Many cars are parked and others queue for a space. All around
the outskirts of the parking area, the ubiquitous and ineradica-
ble *sabr* cacti flourish in massive clusters. The cacti are living

markers, arboreal reminders of some five-hundred Palestinian villages depopulated and destroyed in the 1948 War for Palestine. There are television crews, camera-people, journalists with notepads and microphones, two men at a slight remove from the throng stand waving large Israeli flags. They protest silently the public ceremony and ritual place-marking walk we will conduct there. Later, another man will follow us — a Jewish, South African immigrant to Israel we assume from his English accent, thick with "Seth Efricanisms" — heckling, yelling, and disrupting the ritual procession of walking through the forest. The walk will be punctuated by stops of collective place-marking at the ruins of place that were, until recently, part of the everyday life of Lubya as home in the world. There, yellow signposts will be erected, re-signing the name of the ruined structures and scattered remnants of Lubya in Arabic, Hebrew, and English. Reinscriptions of an erased toponomy on a ruined topography. Walking amidst ruins. The spring sun punishes our heads as we wait in the gathering area beside the parked cars while greetings are shared between friends and families and between associates and comrades from a range of civil formations, who have traveled from Haifa, Deir Hanna, Taybeh, Nazareth, as well as from Tel Aviv, Jerusalem, and much, much further away. But I am jumping ahead. Let me back up and dwell a little on the overlaid, entangled topographies and discursively segregated toponomies that are the reason for our unlikely group to convene here. For the ceremony at Lubya brought together an unusual configuration of geographically dispersed yet historically connected participants in a joint memory action connected to the *topos.* The contours of this experimental and unprecedented action may sketch a way to consider how a transnational or even non-national, civil practice of solidarity could emerge from disparate, "multidirectional,"[1] if uneasy, memories of injustices perpetrated in the name of ethno-nationalism.

---

1   Michael Rothberg, *Multidirectional Memory: Remembering the Holocaust in the Age of Decolonization* (Stanford: Stanford University Press, 2009).

Critical studies on the politics of memory have drawn attention to the historical entanglements and discursive transactions of geographically, historically, and generationally separated experiences of annihilatory violence. In tracking these through visual arts and literature, Marianne Hirsch, through her influential concept of postmemory, elaborates the multi-sited and multi-layered travels of intergenerational and transnational inheritances of the Holocaust. For Hirsch, postmemory emerges through the visual arts as a question that is often familial in its tropes and gendered in its aesthetic vocabularies.[2] Michael Rothberg re-imagines memory politics along a somewhat related trajectory with his critique of the zero-sum or competitive approach to public memory for its logic of scarcity. If anything, the traffic between public memories of the Holocaust and those of anticolonial wars, slavery, and similar historical experiences of collective suffering is much more fluid, dynamic, and layered than the territorializing and exclusionary approach to memory that the zero-sum game suggests.[3] Rothberg's concept of multidirectional memory elaborates an idea connecting the Shoah to memories of decolonization, apartheid South Africa — and to which I would add the Palestine *Nakba* — as "conjunctural effects of world historical events."[4] Hirsch and Rothberg's work, amongst others', highlight the political and ethical stakes of memory formations. Directionality, multi- or uni-, is a thoroughly spatial concept. Excavations of the complex, discursive layers and heterochronous dimensions of time at work in interconnected practices of remembrance may often, through the spatialization of memory practices, produce further political

2   Marianne Hirsch, *Family Frames: Photography, Narrative and Postmemory* (Cambridge: Harvard University Press, 1997). See also Marianne Hirsch, *The Generation of Postmemory: Writing and Visual Culture After the Holocaust* (New York: Columbia University Press, 2012).

3   Michael Rothberg, "Trauma Theory, Implicated Subjects, and the Question of Israel/Palestine," MLA *Profession,* May 2014, https://profession.mla.org/trauma-theory-implicated-subjects-and-the-question-of-israel-palestine/.

4   Michael Rothberg, "Rethinking the Politics of the Past: Multidirectional Memory in the Archives of Implication," in *Marking Evil: Holocaust Memory in the Global Age,* eds. Amon Goldberg and Haim Hazan (New York: Berghahn Books, 2015), 212.

and ethical fault lines. While the work of these scholars to inflect conceptions of memory with less static and more fluid and non-national sensibilities, the strange and insistent call of Mnemosyne to collectively respond to great injustice continues to be spatially imagined in nationalist paradigms and territorialized politics.

In responding to the mass displacements and expulsions inflicted on Palestinians, at very least since 1947 or '48, and to the excision of Palestinians from Israel's topography, toponymy, and narratives of the past, a question arises: how could ethical demands for acknowledgement, place-marking, preservation of ruins, and struggles for restitution and return be spatialized in ways that are inflected with the historical entanglements and multidirectional sensibilities that have shaped their conditions of possibility? The question is sharpened when considering Esmail Nashif's insight into the constitutive relationship of memory to forgetting, a contradiction that is sharpened in light of the power of an ethnic nationalist state to forcefully shape both terms. "There is a serious problem with memory and language," Nashif writes. "Instead of making ruins present, memory effaces them. In Palestinian discourse, the ruins pass through this sort of thick curtain and appear merely as something to celebrate."[5]

Arboreal Time and Negations of History

Two years earlier, I had spent time amidst the ruins of Lubya in the strangely arcadian space of the JNF's South Africa Forest[6]

---

5   Esmail Nashif, "Talking Ruins," in *Unmade Film*, eds. Andrea Thal and Uriel Orlow (Zurich: editions fink, 2014), 129.

6   The Jewish National Fund (JNF) was established in 1901 as a land purchase and settlement instrument of the Zionist movement. Mandated to acquire lands in perpetuity in historic Palestine, not for the state but for all Jewish people, the JNF redefined its relationship to the newly established state of Israel following the 1947/1948 war for Palestine becoming a pillar of Israel's land regime holding 13% of Israel's public lands and exerting control over Israel's remaining public lands through the Israel Lands Authority (ILA) on whose board of directors JNF office-bearers hold six of the ILA's thirteen seats. The JNF has been a key institution in "Judaizing" historic Palestine

creating *The Village under the Forest* with Mark J. Kaplan, a film about the making of South Africa Forest — part of a larger forest called, Lavie — and the unmaking of Lubya, the destroyed Palestinian village.[7] The film delves into both spaces of the ruins of Lubya and the forest planted over it from the perspective of the Jewish diaspora in South Africa. JNF tree-planting and forest-sponsorships have played a crucial role in the production of Israeli space in the Jewish diaspora as part of indoctrinating Zionist values and affective and ideological affiliations to Israel — a connection to "the land" — for non-Israeli Jews.[8]

The creation of a modern, political, Zionist version and vision of history has involved two important yet interconnected negations that have accompanied its drive to reshape "facts on the ground," a term that signifies both the symbolic space of discourse, of ideas, cartographic imaginaries, political claims, and moral narratives, as much as it signifies the territorial, physical, and topographical dimensions of coercive place-making. The first is the negation of the historicity of the Jewish diaspora and its multiple heterogeneous pasts especially through the Arab World, Africa, Europe, and the Americas.[9] Reducing the heterogeneous histories of Jewish life to the teleology of the Nazi concentration camp, this negation has functioned as a justifica-

through Jewish settlement, infrastructural, forestation, and other state projects, particularly in areas from which Palestinians had been depopulated and prevented from return.

7   Mark J. Kaplan and Heidi Grunebaum, dir., *The Village under the Forest* (Cape Town: Grey Matter Media, 2013).

8   See Yoram Bar-Gal, *Propaganda and Zionist Education: The Jewish National Fund 1924–1947* (Rochester: University of Rochester Press, 2003). See also Carol Bardenstein, "Threads of Memory and Discourses of Rootedness: Of Trees, Oranges and the Prickly-pear Cactus in Israel/Palestine," *Edebiyât: Journal of Middle Eastern Literatures* 8, no. 1 (1998): 1–36; Irus Braverman, "Planting the Promised Landscape: Zionism, Nature, and Resistance in Israel/Palestine," *Natural Resources Journal* 49, no. 2 (Spring 2009): 317–61.

9   Amnon Raz-Krakotzkin, "Exile and Binationalism: From Gershom Scholem and Hannah Arendt to Edward Said and Mahmoud Darwish." Carl Heinrich Becker Lecture of the Fritz Thyssen Stiftung 2011 (Berlin: Wissenschaftskolleg zu Berlin, 2012).

tory narrative for the Law of Return, one of Israel's Basic Laws which confers automatic, political rights to citizenship to Jewish people to "return," or rather, to "ascend" to "Zion." The second negation is the negation of the collective existence of Palestinians semiotically, historically, and politically. Baruch Kimmerling has called this negation a "politicide" and Ilan Pappé has described it in terms of a "memoricide" — that is, the destruction and replacement of the physical traces of the collective existence of Palestinians expelled prior to and during the 1948 War for Palestine and whose rights to return and restitution of land and property continue to be abrogated.[10] Battles for memory, of which the Lubya and South Africa Forest *topos* is exemplary, unfold on sharply unequal spatial sites of deletion and historical disavowal shaped further by vastly asymmetrical discursive grounds and institutional/archival conditions.

In 2014, in response to our film, *The Village under the Forest,* a group of Jewish South Africans were introduced to Naif Hujjo, a representative of displaced Palestinians from Lubya involved in the film in order to consult about appropriate gestures of response, acknowledgement, and commitment to restitution. Lubya's inhabitants were expelled in 1948, and the village was destroyed to prevent them from returning. Similar instances of conquest, depopulation, and destruction occurred across the land in some 500 villages and urban areas. Lubya's ruins are scattered, buried beneath the JNF South Africa Forest. Many in the Jewish South African group who travelled to the ceremony had contributed pocket money as children to the JNF's "blue boxes," or collection tins, in the belief that we were greening the desert in a land we learned had been unpopulated and uncultivated. The South African group was also put in contact with Zochrot, an Israeli NGO dedicated to bringing the *Nakba* into Israeli social consciousness through social pedagogy, political education

---

10 Baruch Kimmerling, *Politicide: The Real Legacy of Ariel Sharon* (London: Verso, 2006) and Ilan Pappé, *The Ethnic Cleansing of Palestine* (Oxford: Oneworld Publications, 2007). See also Nur Masalha, *The Politics of Denial: Israel and the Palestinian Refugee Problem* (London: Pluto Press, 2003).

and action tours at the sites of destroyed Palestinian villages and urban areas. *Zochrot,* in Hebrew, means "they remember" or "remembering" in the feminine plural form, the least-used verb form in Hebrew. Zochrot's approach to memory activism is premised on a political commitment to bring the Nakba into Jewish Israeli social awareness and to demilitarize Israeli memory narratives which have harnessed the transgenerational effects of the Holocaust. The instrumentalization of the Holocaust in Israeli national memorial narratives works to justify the militarization of everyday life in Israeli society and the ongoing colonization and occupation of Palestinian lives and lands. Israeli nationalist narratives and national commemorative days, also observed in the Jewish diaspora, deploy a collective sense of existential precarity after the Holocaust in order to mobilize the political and military project of the state as one ensuring collective, Jewish "security."

The group was put in touch with ADRID (the Association for the Rights of the Internally Displaced, a Palestinian organization in Israel). ADRID agreed to define and lead the process and, together with Zochrot, to host a joint action at Lubya. For just over a year, long distance discussions were held to plan our visit, aspects of the joint action and a ceremony at the site of the forest and the village. Some Palestinian refugees from Lubya and their descendants living in Scandinavia expressed interest to join the ceremony which they did. Discussions were also held with other Jewish South Africans who had publicly or privately expressed the wish to address their complicity with the concealment of Lubya's remains having directly or indirectly sponsored trees in the JNF forest. The planned joint action and public ceremony would include handing over some two hundred pledges from Jewish South Africans to Palestinians at Lubya. The "Pledge of Solidarity" took the temporal horizon of futures as its reference for memory activism, so as signatories, "apologise for what has been done in our name," they simultaneously "pledge our joint efforts towards public recognition of both the historical realities that have led to [Palestinian] suffering and the need for appropriate reparations and redress."[11]

Non-redemptive Memory and a Procession through the Ruins

Initially planned for August 2014, the ceremony was postponed to May 2015 due to Israel's unprecedented attack on Gaza. The public ceremony took place on May Day 2015. Two days preceding, Palestinians from Lubya, together with the South Africans cleaned the remains of the graves at Lubya's cemetery. There, we listened to stories of exile as shared by the older generation Palestinians from Lubya, as well as stories and anecdotes from decades of civil activism by Palestinian citizens of Israel, such as the events of the 1976 March *Youm al Ard* (Land Day) protests, the annual *Nakba* Day marches which symbolically return to different villages destroyed in the *Nakba,* and other interventions in political, labor, legal, and civil activism.

The shared act of cleansing the desecrated graves at the Lubya cemetery as a gesture of showing care to the living and to the dead, however, warrants much further reflection than I give here. It is worth mentioning thought that the grave cleaning was a deeply moving and emotional activity for the older participants in the Jewish South African group. For us it reminded of the mass graves and of in the forests of Lithuania, Poland, and through Eastern Europe and of Jewish grave desecrations during the Holocaust. But there was a deep discomfort, an uncertainty about the ethical propriety of sharing these associations with our hosts given the centrality of the Holocaust in the militarization of Israeli nationalism and its instrumentalization to justify the oppression of Palestinians. Our personal and familial connections to Holocaust memory felt inadmissible, unfitting even. Cleaning the graves at Lubya was not part of the public ceremony. The ambiguous presence and absence of the Holocaust that some of our group sensed but could not raise sug-

---

11 "My Pledge of Solidarity," in *Remembering Lubya* (Tel Aviv: Zochrot, 2015).

gests that while multi-directional and noncompetitive memory practices are crucial to theorize and engage, they are harder and morally messier to practice. Like the ruins of the destroyed villages, the insistent presence of the sabr cacti, and of pomegranate, almond, and olive trees that continue to grow despite the acidic environment created by the pine forest, arboreal time messes with conventional perceptions of spatial memory. The episodic, the successive, and the discrete: these modes of spatial memorialization of ruins appear absurd when the ruins are imagined, rather, through the time of trees.

The day of the ritual procession and public ceremony began with an assembly of about three hundred people to undertake a collective, walking ritual of place-marking under the direction of Zochrot. Zochrot's memorial booklet published for the joint action was handed out to participants at the gathering point at the forest's parking area. It included English, Arabic, and Hebrew language texts, including one from the South African group alongside a copy of the pledge of which two hundred signed copies were presented to elders from Lubya at the public ceremony. The Jewish South African activist who spoke on behalf of the group at the start of the joint action, invoked the centrality of the stakes of memory as a relational practice at the start of the afternoon's ritual walk through Lubya's ruins and the pledge-sharing ceremony:

Whether we knew it or not, the money that we donated to the JNF bought the seeds that grew into these trees that cover your houses, your wells and your sacred places. While this forest may be an attempt to erase the memory of Lubya, there can be no denying what happened here. These stones, these graves, these wells, these cacti plants are all bearing witness. Now as Jewish South Africans we have come here to this forest and to the ruins of Lubya in order to acknowledge and to take responsibility for this injustice.[12]

12 Zochrot, "Public Apology in the Palestinian Village of Lubya | An Initiative of StopTheJNF South Africa," *YouTube,* September 11, 2018, https://

This address to our hosts raises the question of implicated subjects and of the entwinements of complicity with memory practices. Michael Rothberg's conception of implicated subjects presents an expansive and indirect idea of complicity through being
conscripted into historical relationships that are structural, interconnected, and broader than individual subject positions and
choices.[13] Rothberg's proposition suggests that the "implicated"
subject are we who inherit histories of mass violence which
cannot be subsumed into categories of victim, perpetrator, by-
stander/beneficiary. These inheritances of violence interpolate
us, "speak" on our behalf and in our place. We are therefore
obliged to address them. Complicity, in this sense, suggests the
need for a temporal reorientation of our understanding of the
afterlives of annihilatory violence in which responsibility may
be ascribed to what can be acted upon and worked through in
the present and future, rather than responses angled towards the
past. Indeed, when memory narratives align to discourses on
heritage, memory may be locked into a concept of "the past"
that sanitizes its messy moral and political predicaments and
durational consequences. At the same time there is a dual risk
in thinking about implication which may diminish the political
agency and moral responsibility of subjects by positioning us either as "traumatised victim — subjects as traumatised victims of
history (i.e., We are all victims)" or "as universally complicitous
with historical violence (i.e., We are all accomplices)."[14] To hold
and inhabit this tension to avoid slipping into either position is a
challenge that requires continuous attention, particularly in the
dispersed yet interconnected historical relations raised through
the joint memory action at Lubya.

The walking procession moved through the forest, along the
pathways and roads that constitute the erased village topography

www.youtube.com/watch?v=KJhvgQSrvPc.

13 Rothberg, "Trauma Theory, Implicated Subjects, and the Question of
    Israel/Palestine." See also Rothberg, "Rethinking the Politics of the Past."

14 Debarati Sanyal, *Memory and Complicity: Migrations of Holocaust Remem-
    brance* (New York: Fordham University Press, 2015), 12.

Fig. 1. Procession. © 2015 Frank Ostyn. Reproduced with kind permission of the photographer.

and that were recalled and re-inscribed through our movement, from one stop to another through the ruins of Lubya (fig. 1).

A temporary community of ceremonial walkers was constituted through the procession of marking erased places of Lubya. The movement of walking together could not but remind me of the terrified flight of the generation of Palestinians made into refugees, often stateless. It recalled in the movement of our bodies and vastly different personal associations, the procession of refugees away from the village in 1948, the terror and uncertainty about where to go, how to survive in a state of homelessness that displacement entailed. Here, in this reversal of that earlier procession of flight, a rehearsal of ingathering and return was inscribed by our ceremonial walk of recollection, narration, and place-marking amidst forest and ruins.

To "return" to Lubya is not to return to an empty space, for the ruins are also traces of intention that they be buried, wiped out, forgotten, leaving no means of return and nowhere to return to. The ruins cannot be celebrated, Esmail Nashif declares.[15]

---

15 Esmail Nashif, "Talking Ruins."

The stops were at the ruins of what had been public buildings and communal sites during Lubya's centuries of habitation, and at each station Zochrot's bright yellow signposts in Arabic, Hebrew, and English were erected. The act of marking and naming the places connected Palestinians from Lubya, their scattered descendants, our Jewish South African group, and the Jewish Israelis. These gestures also linked those present to the materiality of history and place in vastly different ways indexed by having sponsored trees in the JNF's pine tree plantation and returning to Lubya's ruins respectively. The gestures of placing the bright yellow signposts made visible and public the connections between past and present across time and dispersed geographies, between heterogeneous modes of social memories and a shared collective commitment to restitution and return — not as an abstract right but a practical rehearsal of the necessary and the possible. In this view, the experimental joint memory practice offers a relational view of return; a view of restitution that locates us all in different ways in widening but interconnected networks tied to the structurally entwined yet historically segregated spatial arrangement of Lubya's ruins and the JNF forest.

Minor Acts in Partitioned Space

In a critical examination of memory activism and the production of space in Palestine-Israel, Noam Leshem notes that while the three central tropes of Israeli social memory — the Shoah, the negation of the Jewish diaspora, and the 1948 War for Palestine as a war of independence — have been vigorously critiqued by critical scholars, less attention has been paid to the relation between the making of space and the Israeli memorial complex.[16] Leshem's analysis is instructive to think about pos-

---

16 I am not sure that I share this assessment since many scholars have emphasised the interconnection of memory to place in the topographical remaking of Israel's landscape involving legal, cartographic, architectural, and discursive erasures. See, for example, Meron Benvenisti, *Sacred Landscape: The Buried History of the Holy Land since 1948,* trans. Maxine Kaufman-Lacusta (Berkeley: University of California Press, 2000); Nadia

sibilities for solidarities that may include non-national and non-redemptive modes of memory activism. If the modern project of political Zionism has connected the negations of Palestinians and historicity of the Jewish diaspora, what possibilities and fields of meaning may open when Palestinians from the Palestinian diaspora, Palestinian citizens of Israel and Jews from the Jewish diaspora convened to ritually walk through and sign-post the ruins of Lubya? What are the implications of thinking about the counter-memory action at Lubya as both de-territori-alizing and re-territorializing the place of memory differently? Leshem turns to Gilles Deleuze and Félix Guattari's reading of Franz Kafka's work as a Minor Literature and suggests that Zochrot's practice of signposting the Nakba villages within the 1949 boundaries of Israel be thought as a Minor Praxis along the lines of Deleuze and Guattari's concept of a Minor Literature. The minor act, Leshem argues, operates in similar ways within the contingencies of highly circumscribed, overdetermined discursive and symbolic space and of the political immediacies and constraints of the inscription or text. In an inherently collective gesture, the minor act may deterritorialize language and re-place or re-territorialize so as to defamiliarize the inscription, interrupting its prior effects and trajectories of meaning opening new possible fields of political action.[17]

Many texts and intertexts supplemented the procession and ceremony at Lubya, in addition to the transient community of practice convened through the joint action. Zochrot published a

Abu El-Haj, *Facts on the Ground: Archaeological Practice and Territorial Self-fashioning in Israeli Society* (Chicago: University of Chicago Press, 2001). Furthermore, see Oren Yiftachel, *Ethnocracy: Land and Identity Politics in Israel/Palestine* (Philadelphia: University of Pennsylvania Press, 2006); Eyal Weizman, *Hollow Land: Israel's Architecture of Occupation* (London and New York: Verso, 2007); and Nur Masalha, *The Palestine Nakba: Decolonising History, Narrating the Subaltern, Reclaiming Memory* (London: ZED, 2012).

17 Noam Leshem, "Memory Activism: Reclaiming Spatial Histories in Israel," in *The Politics of Cultural Memory,* eds. Lucy Burke, Simon Faulkner, and Jim Aulich (Newcastle upon Tyne: Cambridge Scholars Publishing, 2010), 158–82.

memorial booklet for the memory action, *Remembering Lubya* in Arabic, Hebrew, and English. The booklet includes an essay by Naif Hujjo, a representative of Lubya's displaced inhabitants. It included a testimonial narrative, an essay by the Jewish South African group, a Zochrot essay on Lubya before it was depopulated and destroyed — in oral histories, nineteenth-century travelogues, Ottoman and British mandatory archives. And it includes a copy of the "Pledge of Solidarity," aesthetically resonant of the generic, JNF tree-planting certificates that sponsors receive from the JNF yet with subtly revised visual elements that undo, estrange, and recast the JNF's certificates and the claims they represent. The booklets were handed out to participants at the gathering point at the forest's parking area and are available online at Zochrot's website. Zochrot's memorial booklet is also a palimpsest of sorts, much like the *topos* itself. It was published in the wakes of the journal *Al Majdal*'s special issue on the JNF (2010) (on whose cover appeared an image of a well in Lubya's ruins and the South African Forest), of Naif Hujjo's memorial book in Arabic on Lubya (1993), and of Mahmoud Issa's legacy, a social historian of Lubya, who was historical consultant to *The Village under the Forest,* the film I made with Mark Kaplan (fig. 2).[18]

After the ceremonial procession of place-marking, the second part of the ceremony took on a different performative sensibility. The ceremonial space was set up in an area at the bottom of a hill below the formerly built area of Lubya and set back from yet next to a wide sand road. Plastic chairs were placed in this area facing the road where the rituals of the ceremony were conducted. It comprised speeches by representatives of ADRID and of Zochrot, singing and handing over of a pledge signed by two hundred other Jewish South Africans to elders from Lubya. The pledge was read aloud by one of the younger members of the South African group. The event was closed with the sing-

---

18 Mahmoud Issa, *Lubya var en landsby I Palæstina: Erindringer, Historie, Kultur, Identitet* (Copenhagen: Tiderne Skifter, 2005). See also Kaplan and Grunebaum, *The Village under the Forest.*

Fig. 2. Zochrot booklet cover, by Umar al-Ghubari/zochrot. Rights reserved by all the people who were expelled from their homes.

ing of the Palestinian national anthem to a prerecorded melody played through the sound system of one of the many cars and connected to external speakers. Affirming the signatories' acknowledgement of the Nakba and recognition of the irreparability of Palestinian loss, the pledge articulated an unconditional commitment to the struggle for Palestinian and Israeli freedom premised on the actual return of the refugees and the displaced. If Zionist pedagogies of place have played a powerful role in the Jewish diaspora, shaping a new collective Jewish memory and enlisting affiliation to and identification with this imagined space as an ethnic national homeland, the public pledge-making subverted the territorializing claims which underpin the discursive features of dominant productions of Israeli space.

There is a risk, of course, that such gestural memorial politics of acknowledgement may amount to not much more than paternalistic performances of hugging, apology, and handshaking. This was raised powerfully by the chairperson of ADRID who warned, not unlike Esmail Nashif, that in the context of an ongoing Nakba in real time, such memorial gestures may do more damage than good. That our small gesture was both permitted and hosted by Palestinians and descendants of Lubya is of great significance. Being welcomed and granted permission to join in the action is a reminder that, contrary to ethnic national privilege and the political entitlements of citizenship that Israel's Right of Return Law promises the Jewish diaspora, we were, in fact, the guests. The Palestinian partners who invited and welcomed us were our hosts, an acknowledgement that we were on their land as visitors and in their homes as guests, which structured a relation in which we were the recipients of generosity and hospitality. The Jewish diaspora, this suggests, has to be rethought and reclaimed beyond the nationalist signification and geographic referents to which it has been confined by the Israeli state.

Perhaps not unsurprisingly, but a source of frustration nonetheless, much of the media framing of the ceremony at Lubya centered around "apology" and reconciliation, rather than joint struggle and restitution. Some of the English-language coverage, such as a CNN video clip and Haaretz newspaper article, framed the joint-memory action in terms that were evocative of the much contested South African Truth and Reconciliation Commission (TRC). These used the language of apology and reconciliation, the "forgive and forget" approach to history that has become stubbornly entrenched in the international narrative of South Africa's post-apartheid scenario. Despite the failure of the elite-driven project in South Africa, the South African fiction of its "miracle" political transition model, and the forgive-and-forget approach to structural injustice endures as a hegemonic global trope of postwar peace-making. Yet precisely because this enduring fictional trope relies on performing a discursive break with the past, such a framing cannot but crumble upon mild scrutiny from the location in which we were gathered (as it has crumbled in South Africa some twenty-five years after regime change!). After all, the memory action at Lubya was conducted in an ongoing situation of incremental ethnic cleansing, unequal civil rights, creeping occupation, and colonization, compounded and acknowledged subsequently via the Knesset's adoption of the Nation State Law in July 2018 that legally entrenched Jewishness as the exclusive and privileged category of citizenship. The experiment in the 2015 joint-memory action at Lubya inverted the temporal script of the South African TRC narrative flipping its temporal vectors and, as such, organizing an inverted relation of time and place to ethical agency and moral responsibility. Such an approach to the past surfaces a different concept of time, the future-present, for a justice-to-come as the grounds for solidarity. If heterochronous dimensions of time were at work in this shared practice in Lubya's ruins, a different question of future-presents and future-pasts might emerge. It is a question through which moral responsibility, politics, restitution, and the necessary work of imagining futures can be viewed — but always through ruins. To enact Rothberg's idea of multidirectional memory in the context of the joint action at Lubya might then also represent a transient if important challenge to the zero-sum mentality which dominates Jewish-Israeli society and diasporic Jewish perspectives with its coercive pressure to unconditionally conform to a state aligned perspective at all costs.

Historically, Jews and Arabs are not mortal enemies. The zero-sum mentality promotes this politically expedient myth which is nourished by Israel's national narratives as well as by the dominant Islamophobic narrative of Euro-American politics over recent decades. It is a myth whose victims are primarily Palestinian; but also Arab-Jews who may now only describe themselves in these terms at great political and psychological cost, as Iraqi-born scholar, Ella Shohat, explains.[19] It is a myth that Israel unceasingly and disingenuously exploits in its version of "War on Terror." Eurocentric and generalized as a uni-

---

19 Ella Shohat, *On the Arab-Jew, Palestine, and Other Displacements: Selected Writings* (London: Pluto Press, 2017) 1–22.

versal truth which feeds fear and the increased conflation of war and politics, this myth contributes to the evisceration of our imagination to envision desegregation and joint struggle as a condition for justice, peace, and living together. Rather, the status quo has been to embrace the necropolitics at the heart of this myth — that is, a politics of death in which the idea of the future is one of war, ethno-fascist nationalisms, and apocalypse. In this, it must be added a fundamentalist and evangelical Christian theology directly informs the political imaginary of the Palestine-Israel situation.

Israeli scholar and activist, Noa Shaindlinger, has argued that "joint" in "joint struggle" cannot, in the current conditions of struggle and repression, mean "equal partnership, but it does indicate our commitment to and solidarity with the Palestinian struggle for liberation from the shackles of colonialism and apartheid." Affirming that "at the heart of a joint struggle should lie a vision for a just postcolonial society," she argues that this needs to include acknowledgement that "Israeli Jews are rooted there, have a profound sense of belonging and attachment to their place of birth, and that another wave of mass displacement will never be a just solution."[20]

Imperfect, difficult, and sometimes improvised, undertaken with thoughtfulness and self-reflexivity, the initiative continues to connect South African, Palestinian, and Israeli partners with relations to Lubya. As an attempt to respond to our complicity with the Nakba, its erasures and impact on the lives of people as well as its continuities through a commitment the initiative opens a new approach to joint struggle or co-resistance with Palestinians. If this experiment in memory activism may forge new civil discourses and political solidarities founded on a desegregation of different and often transnational memories of mass violence and forced displacements, the tensions and contradictions emerging through our action would need to be considered

---

20 Noa Shaindlinger, "Thoughts on a Joint but Unequal Palestinian-Israeli Struggle," +972 *Magazine,* June 23, 2012, https://www.972mag.com/thoughts-on-a-joint-yet-unequal-palestinian-israeli-liberation-struggle/.

as productive for holding Shaindlinger's proposition in mind. All the more for those like our Jewish South African group who have committed to joint struggle, reimagining solidarity, and its implicit claim to relationship to the Palestinian movement for freedom and equality. Such a relationship can neither ignore the ruins nor celebrate them.

Acknowledgments

I warmly thank the people and organizations who hosted the ceremony at Lubya, notably ADRID and Zochrot. I am deeply grateful for the hospitality extended to my daughter and me during our stay in the Galilee. Finally, I thank the South African group for inviting me to join them accompanied by my daughter in this remarkable joint action.

Bibliography

Abu El-Haj, Nadia. *Facts on the Ground: Archaeological Practice and Territorial Self-fashioning in Israeli Society.* Chicago: University of Chicago Press, 2001.

Bar-Gal, Yoram. *Propaganda and Zionist Education: The Jewish National Fund 1924–1947.* Rochester: University of Rochester Press, 2003.

Bardenstein, Carol. "Threads of Memory and Discourses of Rootedness: Of Trees, Oranges and the Prickly-pear Cactus in Israel/Palestine." *Edebiyât: Journal of Middle Eastern Literatures* 8, no. 1 (1998): 1–36.

Benvenisti, Meron. *Sacred Landscape: The Buried History of the Holy Land since 1948.* Translated by Maxine Kaufman-Lacusta. Berkeley: University of California Press, 2000.

Braverman, Irus. "Planting the Promised Landscape: Zionism, Nature, and Resistance in Israel/Palestine." *Natural Resources Journal* 49, no. 2 (Spring 2009): 317–61. https://www.jstor.org/stable/24889569.

Hirsch, Marianne. *Family Frames: Photography, Narrative and Postmemory.* Cambridge: Harvard University Press, 1997.

Hirsch, Marianne. *The Generation of Postmemory: Writing and Visual Culture after the Holocaust.* New York: Columbia University Press, 2012.

Issa, Mahmoud. *Lubya var en landsby I Palæstina: Erindringer, Historie, Kultur, Identitet.* Copenhagen: Tiderne Skifter, 2005.

———. "Resisting Oblivion: Historiography of the Destroyed Palestinian Village of Lubya." *Refuge* 21, no. 2 (2003): 14–22. DOI: 10.25071/1920-7336.21286.

———. "The Nakba, Oral History and the Palestinian Peasantry: The Case of Lubya." In *Catastrophe Remembered: Palestine, Israel and the Internal Refugees, Essays in Memory of Edward W. Said,* edited by Nur Masalha, 178–96. London: ZED, 2005.

"My Pledge of Solidarity." In *Remembering Lubya.* Tel Aviv: Zochrot, 2015.

Kaplan, Mark J., and Heidi Grunebaum, dir. *The Village under the Forest*. Cape Town: Grey Matter Media, 2013, DVD.

Kimmerling, Baruch. *Politicide: The Real Legacy of Ariel Sharon*. London: Verso, 2006.

Leshem, Noam. "Memory Activism: Reclaiming Spatial Histories in Israel." In T*he Politics of Cultural Memory*, edited by Lucy Burke, Simon Faulkner, and Jim Aulich, 158–82. Newcastle upon Tyne: Cambridge Scholars Publishing, 2010.

Masalha, Nur. *The Palestine Nakba: Decolonising History, Narrating the Subaltern, Reclaiming Memory*. London: ZED Books, 2012.

———. *The Politics of Denial: Israel and the Palestinian Refugee Problem*. London: Pluto Press, 2003.

Nashif, Esmail. "Talking Ruins." In *Unmade Film,* edited by Andrea Thal and Uriel Orlow, 123–232. Zurich: editions fink, 2014.

Pappé, Ilan. *The Ethnic Cleansing of Palestine*. Oxford: Oneworld Publications, 2007.

Raz-Krakotzkin, Amnon. "Exile and Binationalism: From Gershom Scholem and Hannah Arendt to Edward Said and Mahmoud Darwish." Carl Heinrich Becker Lecture of the Fritz Thyssen Stiftung 2011. Berlin: Wissenschaftskolleg zu Berlin, 2012.

Rothberg, Michael. *Multidirectional Memory: Remembering the Holocaust in the Age of Decolonization*. Stanford: Stanford University Press, 2009.

Rothberg, Michael. "Trauma Theory, Implicated Subjects, and the Question of Israel/Palestine." *MLA Profession,* May 2014. https://profession.mla.org/trauma-theory-implicated-subjects-and-the-question-of-israel-palestine/.

———. "Rethinking the Politics of the Past: Multidirectional Memory in the Archives of Implication." In *Marking Evil: Holocaust Memory in the Global Age,* edited by Amos Goldberg and Haim Hazan, 211–29. New York: Berghahn Books, 2015.

Sanyal, Debarati. *Memory and Complicity: Migrations of Holocaust Remembrance.* New York: Fordham University Press, 2015.

Shaindlinger, Noa. "Thoughts on a Joint But Unequal Palestinian-Israeli Struggle." *+972 Magazine,* June 23, 2012. https://www.972mag.com/thoughts-on-a-joint-yet-unequal-palestinian-israeli-liberation-struggle/.

Shohat, Ella. *On the Arab-Jew, Palestine, and Other Displacements: Selected Writings.* London: Pluto Press, 2017.

Weizman, Eyal. *Hollow Land: Israel's Architecture of Occupation.* London and New York: Verso, 2007.

Yiftachel, Oren. *Ethnocracy: Land and Identity Politics in Israel/Palestine.* Philadelphia: University of Pennsylvania Press, 2006.

Zochrot. "Public Apology in the Palestinian Village of Lubya | An Initiative of StopTheJNF South Africa." *YouTube,* September 11, 2018. https://www.youtube.com/watch?v=KJhvgQSrvPc.

2

Materiality

Alexandra Binnenkade & Felicitas Macgilchrist

Scene 1, Autumn 2018. The German astronaut Alexander Gerst assumes command of the International Space Station (ISS). Kids across Germany, including one six-year-old boy, son of one of this chapter's authors, go wild. In the kitchen of his home, YouTube endlessly plays the boy's favorite song, Peter Schilling's "Major Tom," featuring Ed Harris as John Glenn, the first American astronaut to go into space. We sing as we watch him take off in the Friendship 7 spacecraft in 1962. This Friendship 7 on the iPad screen is part of the disorderly materiality of Lego astronauts, Playmobil rockets, tinfoil-covered cardboard box rockets, old and new books about space travel. Some books, translations from the English, place the moon landing and Neil Armstrong in prime, memorial position. Others, German books, East German books, foreground the stories of Sigmund Jähn, the first German cosmonaut, and Yuri Gagarin. Different objects undergird different stories. Different technologies are pictured and explained. Different arrays of materiality support the Cold-War Space Race tales as they reverberate in children's rooms today.

Scene 2, Winter 2017. At the same kitchen table, two authors start writing a chapter on memory. Their online research takes them to a series of objects related to the Friendship 7 capsule of the Mercury-Atlas 6 spaceflight. Many of these are preserved in memory institutions, such as the Air and Space Museum on the National Mall in Washington, DC, others can be found in technologies of memory like YouTube, where the authors listen to Gil Scott-Heron's "Whitey on the Moon." The authors find themselves in a transnational trickbox of things which connect to the same monumentalized event: the USA's first manned orbital flight. In regard to their function for Cold-War memory politics, these material objects stand on equal terms with written reports or historiography about the event. But it is still uncommon to consider "things" from this perspective. The authors talk to each other about the concatenations of materializations and propaganda which unfold and fold up bodies, character traits, connectivity, fuel, nationalism, progress, and the Space Race into this one capsule. The online accessibility of the material objects is crucial for this to happen. The authors realize the potential of taking a closer look at the connections among these material elements, swirling in and around the Friendship 7 capsule, for their purpose. But before engaging more closely with the capsule, they want to contextualize their perspective on materiality. They know where to start: British Columbia.

Scene 3, Spring 2012. Erin Gibson, an ethnographer, arrives in the Southwest of British Columbia, Canada, between Port Douglas to the South and the Lillooet Lake in the North, to research a special road. This road was built in 1859 to provide miners and merchants with a less dangerous route to travel to the Fraser Canyon, the location of the Fraser River Gold Rush. It replaced a pack trail, built in 1858, that is believed to have followed the route of a preexisting First Nations (Indigenous) trail.[1] When Gibson arrived in the area, she assumed that the road was remembered by the Stl'atl'imx people as part of a colonizing power structure, associated with the dispossession of their land and subjugation of their people.[2] But to her surprise she discovered that the wagon road was regarded with pride, as-

---

1   Erin L.S. Gibson, "Remembering Tomorrow: Wagon Roads, Identity and the Decolonization of a First Nations Landscape," *Public History Review* 23 (2016): 27.

2   Ibid., 28.

sociated with Stl'atl'limx ancestors, community, and tradition. Members of the community had maintained this road over the years and thus physically and socially turned it into a memory object of their own. The place, the road as material object, as Gibson found out, was now the touchstone of different relationships with the past. Material touchstones are important in their own right, and they are also integrated into experiences, procedures, and practices.

Scene 4, Winter 1909. When the trapper arrived at the Berkeley's Museum of Vertebrate Zoology, he not only carried a dead animal in his bag but along with it came the experience and history of living outdoors, the trapper's concept of nature, his social and economic life-world, and the understanding of this animal as prey and trading good. Later, when the biologist decided what taxonomic group to ascribe the animal to, he was acting within a scientific framework, led by a set of procedures for collecting and curating specimen.[3] He held conceptions of nature that were different from the trapper's, even though they probably overlapped at certain points since both men were members of a white, Christian-American culture of their time. Concerned about meeting professional standards, the biologist would soon prefer to engage fieldmen for his purpose. These men worked more systematically than trappers or other people who brought in specimen at random occasions. The fieldmen knew how to document animals in a particular place at a certain time of day and season of the year.[4] The animal's body was a material object that came to mean different things in different worlds. It was a key participant in an iterative network of meanings, of translations, transactions, and representations. It was for these characteristics that the dead animal's body became a specimen in a museum collection, and it became a meaningful research object about the past.

---

3   Susan Leigh Star and James R. Griesemer, "Institutional Ecology, 'Translations' and Boundary Objects: Amateurs and Professionals in Berkeley's Museum of Vertebrate Zoology, 1907–39," *Social Studies of Science* 19, no. 3 (August 1989): 395.

4   Ibid., 398.

Since Leigh Star's work on different memory practices in the museum in 1989 to more recent work on material memory such as Gibson's ethnographic work and the memory scholars' kitchen-table reflections on the multiple accumulations of materiality around the spacecraft, scholarly interest has grown in what materiality "does" in regards to memory and in how memory is entangled with not only texts and meanings but also material things and practices.[5] Objects can relate past, present, and future, combine different perspectives and meanings. They are marked by differentiation: "Boundaries are drawn by mapping practices; 'objects' do not pre-exist as such. Objects are boundary projects."[6] However, as Mieke Bal stated in *Double Exposures,* objects, although present, are "mute." They are bound into relations of agency, but they have no stable, inherent meaning, they only "come to mean."[7] Going one step further, the question for Karen Barad was not only how meaning is made, but, more fundamentally, also how matter is made. For Barad, "matter and meaning are mutually articulated. Neither discursive practices nor material phenomena are ontologically or epistemologically prior. Neither can be explained in terms of the other. Neither has privileged status in determining the other."[8] Although material objects are physically, visibly, audibly present, it becomes "impossible to differentiate in any absolute sense between crea-

---

5   For more on materiality and memory, see, for instance, Paul Connerton, *How Societies Remember* (Cambridge: Cambridge University Press, 1995); Geoffrey C. Bowker, *Memory Practices in the Sciences* (Cambridge: MIT Press, 2008); Geoffrey C. Bowker, "All Knowledge Is Local," *Learning Communities* (2008): 138–49; and Elizabeth Anderson et al., *Memory, Mourning, Landscape* (Amsterdam: Rodopi: 2010).

6   Donna J. Haraway, "Situated Knowledges: The Science Question in Feminism and the Privilege of Partial Perspective," *Feminist Studies* 14, no. 3 (Fall 1988): 595.

7   Mieke Bal, *Double Exposures: The Practice of Cultural Analysis* (New York: Routledge, 1996), 4.

8   Karen Barad, "Posthumanist Performativity: Toward an Understanding of How Matter Comes to Matter," *Signs: Journal of Women in Culture and Society* 28, no. 3 (Spring 2003): 822.

tion and renewal, beginning and returning, continuity and discontinuity, here and there, past and future."⁹

The insight that objects are polysemic is not new.¹⁰ We are repeating it with established and current scholarship in order to explore where this perspective can take us when we study memory practices. An increasing number of scholars is now thinking memory practices with materiality, with objects' material qualities and those material qualities' histories.¹¹ What gains can be made if we focus on the intra-activity of materiality in memory? In the realm of memory, objects tend to be made monovocal, monocontextual, monocultural. In our own research we are looking for ways in which such apparent closeness can be blasted. This chapter thus engages with materiality and material objects as open, uncertain and multiple. To do this, we read their "coming to mean," or their "becoming," *simultaneously in different contexts.* Contextualization is our key method, our "prosthetic device," for "try[ing] to strike up non-innocent conversations," by, for instance, finding stories that have been marginalized in hegemonic modes of memory-making, whether we agree with their perspectives or not; and we hope to make apparently incommensurable positions legible to one another.¹² Contextualization enables us to tell stories about politics, affects, and values and to list contexts which seem contradictory.

Overall, our aim in this chapter is quite straightforward. We want to pick up Donna Haraway's observation that when you

9 Karen Barad, *Meeting the Universe Halfway: Quantum Physics and the Entanglement of Matter and Meaning* (Durham: Duke University Press, 2007), ix.
10 Marzia Varutti, "Polysemic Objects and Partial Translations: Museums and the Interpretation of Indigenous Material Culture in Taiwan," *Museum Anthropology* 37, no. 2 (September 2014): 102–17.
11 A whole conference was, for instance, devoted to the nexus of memory, materiality and visuality in 2016, "Making Memory: Visual and Material Cultures of Commemoration in Ireland," see the program at https://makingmemoryconference.wordpress.com. Tracy Ireland and Jane Lydon, "Rethinking Materiality, Memory and Identity," *Public History Review* 23 (2016): 1–8.
12 Haraway, "Situated Knowledges," 597.

stroke one individual dog, you touch also the histories, the materialities, the connections and webs of material-semiotic entities making it up.[13] And also Elizabeth St. Pierre's joy when she
"imagine[s] a cacophony of ideas swirling as we think about
our topics with all we can muster — with words from theorists,
participants, conference audiences, friends and lovers, ghosts
who haunt our studies, characters in fiction and film and
dreams — and with our bodies and all the other bodies and the
earth and all the things and objects in our lives — the entire assemblage that is a *life* thinking *and, and, and...*"[14]

We take one object — the Mercury Atlas Rocket (fig. 1) — and
ask where it takes us. We follow multiple flows and connections
in which it has been, and can be, contextualized. Rather than
thinking of "this *or* that," "this, *but* that," we are thinking here of
"this *and* that."[15] The and "is neither a union nor a juxtaposition,
but the birth of a stammering, the outline of a broken line which
always sets off at right angles, a sort of active and creative line of
flight."[16] In accounting for multiple contexts, we want to make it
"possible to manage things by doing both [or many] at the same
time" by transversal movements that destabilize neat binaries
and categorizations.[17]

---

13 Donna J. Haraway, *Companion Species Manifesto: Dogs, People, and Signifi-
    cant Otherness* (Chicago: Prickly Paradigm Press, 2003), 98.

14 Elizabeth A. St. Pierre, "Post Qualitative Research: The Critique and
    the Coming After," in *The Sage Handbook of Qualitative Research,* eds.
    Norman K. Denzin and Yvonna S. Lincoln, 4th edn. (Los Angeles: Sage
    Publications, 2011), 621.

15 We are certain we have read an article with this idea, but we are unable to
    source the quotes. We thank the writer(s), and ask them to let us know if
    they recognize their words.

16 Gilles Deleuze and Claire Parnet, *Dialogues II,* trans. Hugh Tomlinson and
    Barbara Habberjam (London: Continuum, 2002), 7.

17 Helen Verran, *Science and an African Logic* (Chicago: University of
    Chicago Press, 2001), 19. For more on doing many memories at the same
    time, see Michael Rothberg, *Multidirectional Memory: Remembering the
    Holocaust in the Age of Decolonization* (Stanford: Stanford University
    Press, 2009). For more on the AND and on drawing on Deleuze as creative
    methodology, see Brooke A. Hofsess and Jennifer L. Sonenberg, "Enter:
    Ho/rhizoanalysis," *Cultural Studies ↔ Critical Methodologies* 13, no. 4

Fig. 1. Glenn enters Friendship 7, the capsule in the Mercury-Atlas 6 spaceflight (1962). Source: NASA *Image Galleries,* July 18, 2011, https://www.nasa.gov/multimedia/imagegallery/image_feature_2009.html.

The textual form that fits these thoughts best and can grasp the cacophony around the memory of the Mercury-Atlas 6 rocket in the space of this chapter is the list. We thus chose to first offer a provisional list and will return at the end of the chapter to reflect on where this list takes us, politically, ethically, methodically, joyfully, multidirectionally, and, and, and.[18]

Bodies

There is this white, phallic body of the rocket and the round, scarred body of the capsule with its time enduring aura of a thing that has been to a place beyond the world and back.

(2013): 299–308. Anja Kanngieser, "… And … and … and … The Transversal Politics of Performative Encounters," *Deleuze Studies* 6, no. 2 (April 2012): 265–90.

18 John Law et al., "Modes of Syncretism: Notes on Non-coherence," CRESC *Working Paper* 119 (2013).

And there is John Glenn's body, the measure after which the bodysuit and the capsule were built. His body was also the object of scientists' quest for the influence of weightlessness on the human, the testing opportunity for drugs under such conditions. And particularly, it was the object that needed to be saved after landing. His white peers from the engineering labs had foreseen different outcomes and thus taken into account that the capsule could land in water. Thus the capsule carried a number of items to secure Glenn's survival, like a shark chase or a whistle, things that marked his body as in peril under all conditions. While always remaining an individual body that had to support the heat and was sweating considerably, one that had to know and physically conduct flight maneuvers under stress, a male body which used humor as a sign of endurance and strength and American-ness; this body also became a deindividualized symbol, a token of the collective, national, Western, capitalist success of a society defined as white. And for this reason, it had to be saved and preserved in order to be shown.

And there were those bodies who decided, financed, wanted and did not want to support the Mercury mission — bodies that invented, computed, constructed, hammered, welded, cleaned, and moved the rocket. These bodies were as raced and gendered as Glenn's. These were people identified as belonging to different groups of age and class, locally engaged, nationally ignored. Later there was a poem by Gil Scott-Heron, "Whitey on the Moon," reflecting on the taxes which fund space travel in the USA in the midst of racialized poverty.[19]

A rat done bit my sister Nell
With whitey on the moon
Her face and arms began to swell
And whitey's on the moon

---

19   Gil Scott-Heron, "Whitey on the Moon," on *Small Talk at 125th and Lenox* (Ace Records Ltd, 1970), vinyl disc, avilable online at Ace Records Ltd, "Gil Scott-Heron - Whitey On the Moon (Official Audio)," *YouTube,* August 19, 2014, https://www.youtube.com/watch?v=goh2x_Goct4.

I can't pay no doctor bills
But whitey's on the moon
Ten years from now I'll be payin' still
While whitey's on the moon.

And then there was a book, written by Margot Lee Shetterly, turned into a film in 2016, co-written with Allison Schroeder, and directed by Theodore Melfi.[20] *Hidden Figures* narrated black, female bodies of mathematicians and engineers back into national memory discourse. By doing so *Hidden Figures* exposed the whiteness, the hegemonic memory discourse, and the social tensions that had materialized the spaceship but that had remained invisible in public remembrance. The film, which shows Katherine Johnson calculating its landing, made Friendship 7 come to mean something different in the US public by opening a context that had been present primarily among African-American members of the NASA community.

Character

The story of the Atlas rocket series from the 1950s to the present is one of the central exhibits at the San Diego Air & Space Museum. At the time of writing, the Atlas exhibit sits alongside "Be the Astronaut," which is described as "a fun, interactive adventure where you are in control as you launch a rocket, pilot a spaceship, and drive a rover in space! [...] *Be the Astronaut* is fun for the whole family and takes STEM [Science, Technology, Engineering, and Math] learning into outer space!"[21] Its "goal is to inspire while it educates and to create a new kind of visitor

20 Margot Lee Shetterly, *Hidden Figures: The American Dream and the Untold Story of the Black Women Mathematicians Who Helped Win the Space Race* (New York: William Morrow Paperbacks, 2016). Theodore Melfi, dir., *Hidden Figures* (Los Angeles: 20th Century Fox, 2016).
21 "Be the Astronaut Opening in February," *San Diego Air & Space Museum,* 2017, http://sandiegoairandspace.org/newsletters/article/be-the-astronaut-opening-in-february

experience."[22] The museum hosts an annual Hall of Fame Gala, celebrating significant honorees under the flag "Legends of Flight." Since 1963, over 200 honorees have been selected, whose "individual contributions are prime examples of endurance and the adventurous exploring spirit in the pursuit of knowledge and scientific advancement to benefit the world."[23] In 2017 honorees include "the Pioneers who made possible the first launch of the revolutionary Atlas missile, sixty years ago."[24]

In these descriptions, the Mercury-Atlas 6 spacecraft, Friendship 7, comes to mean within the contemporary, international language of "psycho-policy," in which educational experiences are explicitly oriented to non-cognitive learning and the shaping of personal character and mindset.[25] In the 1960s, the Space Race was part of a broader Cold-War agenda including CIA-sponsored research on behavior control.[26] Today, the 1960s spacecraft is placed in a web of very particular, economically useful behaviors and character traits such as endurance and a pioneering, adventurous, exploring spirit. Young people learn to see labor as fun, adventurous, and inspirational. The exhibition signals to visitors that they (are expected to) want to be in control. The memory of Atlas is folded into emerging educational policies and practices, where socio-emotional learning is becoming a core strategy for managing children's behavior. Atlas thus also shapes more generally what counts as the good life in today's world.

22 Ibid.

23 "2017 International Air & Space Induction Celebration Set for Nov. 9," *San Diego Air & Space Museum,* 2017, http://sandiegoairandspace.org/blog/article/2017-international-air-space-induction-celebration-set-for-nov.-9.

24 Ibid.

25 Ben Williamson, "Decoding ClassDojo: Psycho-policy, Social-emotional Learning and Persuasive Educational Technologies," *Learning, Media and Technology* 42, no. 4 (January 2017): 440–53.

26 Nancy Campbell, quoted in Donna J. Haraway, *Modest_Witness@Second_Millenium. FemaleMan.©Meets_OncoMouse™: Feminism and Technoscience* (New York: Routledge, 1997), 280.

Connectivity

Searching for #friendship7 on Instagram, we find 1,256 posts. Among them are images of a young woman and a child in front of the capsule (#lovehim, #myson, #blackandwhite), of the NASA Mercury Mission Control Room "as it was in 1962" (#kennedyspacecenter, #spaceage), of an arm with a tattoo, "Friendship 7, Mercury 6, Glenn" (#NASA, #ChapelTattooEST1994), of out-of-focus black and white photos of Dorothy Vaughan, Katherine Johnson, and Mary Jackson (#hiddenfigures, #fairnessandequality), and of a gif of a new beer brewed by the Launch Pad Brewery (#newlabel, #hero, #spacepioneers, #craftbeerisourrocketfuel).

In our culture of connectivity, digital images shared on social media contribute to a dynamic visual archive of how objects, such as the Friendship 7 spacecraft, come to mean within networks of personal and collective remembering. These images and platforms are also firmly embedded in "a culture where the powerful structures of social networking sites are gradually penetrating the core of our daily routines and practices."[27] As we have access to new apps, larger data storage, and faster processors, our socio-technical memory practices are also changing. This brings forth enthusiasm for the "increasingly digital networking of memory," which "not only functions in a continuous present but is also a distinctive shaper of a new mediatised age of memory."[28] And it also brings forth concerns about the co-opting of people's unpaid labor as they produce the memory images which advertise, for instance, the Kennedy Space Center or the National Air & Space Museum, and as personal images related to the spacecraft generate the big data that fuel the social media companies' revenues.

---

27 José van Dijck, "Flickr and the Culture of Connectivity: Sharing Views, Experiences, Memories," *Memory Studies* 4, no. 4 (October 2011): 401.

28 Andrew Hoskins, "Digital Network Memory," in *Mediation, Remediation, and the Dynamics of Cultural Memory,* eds. Ann Rigney and Astrid Erll (Berlin: de Gruyter, 2009), 96.

Fuel

When the capsule started its first orbit, it carried a fuel supply of 60.4 pounds (27.4 kilograms), 36 pounds (16.3 kilograms) for the automatic control system, and 24.4 pounds (11.1 kilograms) for the manual control system.

"Glenn noticed the control problem when the automatic stabilization and control system allowed the spacecraft to drift about a degree and a half per second to the right. Glenn switched control to manual-proportional control mode and moved Friendship 7 back to the proper attitude. He tried different control modes to see which used the least fuel to maintain attitude. The manual fly-by-wire combination used the least fuel. [...] While he was still over Australia, another warning light came on, indicating that the fuel supply for the automatic control system was down to sixty-two percent. Mercury Control recommended that Glenn let the spacecraft attitude drift to conserve fuel. [...] (After reentry) The spacecraft control system was working well but the manual fuel supply was down to fifteen percent. The peak of reentry deceleration was still to come. [...] The astronaut could not control the ship manually (anymore). The spacecraft was oscillating past ten degrees on both sides of the vertical zero-degree point. 'I felt like a falling leaf,' Glenn later said. [... But manual steering was not advisable anymore, because] Fuel in the automatic tanks was getting low. [...] The automatic fuel supply ran out at one minute and fifty-one seconds, and manual fuel ran out at fifty-one seconds, before drogue chute deployment."[29]

In the context of this English Wikipedia account of the Apollo-Mercury 6 mission, Friendship 7's fuel comes to be a pivotal agent of drama and suspense. It is through fuel that crucial questions are narrated: Would Glenn land safely? Would technology support or impede human intentions? Who would ultimately

---

29 *Wikipedia*, s.v. "Mercury-Atlas 6," https://en.wikipedia.org/w/index. php?title=Mercury-Atlas_6&oldid=810524542.

win: material conditions or Glenn's wit? Would the events be remembered as tragedy or success?

The fuel stages other important elements of the story. Friendship 7 and Glenn were equally monitored and accompanied not only by mission control in Cape Canaveral, Florida. Along with it, tracking stations around the globe co-checked the instruments and fuel supplies. Their capsule communicators connected with the spaceship and one another, forming a tight technospatial network that included Kano, Nigeria; Muchea, Australia; Kauai, Hawaii; Guyamas, Mexico; Zanzibar, Tanzania.

These sites, shaped by colonialism and decolonization movements, representing areas of otherness for the USA, co-created a highly, almost intimately, nationalized US-American event. With Cape Canaveral at the communicative epicenter, the tracking stations represented and highlighted the colonial power structure of the Cold War. The global tracking stations co-created safety through presence, voice, technical expertise. They maintained and generated communication between the orbit, Glenn, and the earth. The narration of this network exhibits the role of the English language as a common denominator among colonized and colonizers (the latter referring to more than the USA).

In a public text where memory is being done, fuel thus suddenly is more than a liquid with specific characteristics, instrumental for the working of the spaceship. It becomes materially, viscerally, dramatically important and comes to mean within a context of colonialism, freedom struggles, and the competing world systems of capitalism and communism.

Nationalism

Friendship 7 and John Glenn completed three orbits. Three months after the landing, Friendship 7 began its second mission, or what was popularly referred to as its "fourth orbit": a worldwide exhibition that was organized to promote and represent the United States and its space program in nearly thirty cities around the world.[30] This tour recalls medieval ruling practices, where effigies of the French king were sent around the country representing him in a form of Real Presence and thus consolidating his power.[31] Real Presence describes the simultaneity of a material object and the mostly sacred power of an absent figure, often a saint.

Even though in fact a *reliquia,* a left-behind object with great signifying powers, the Friendship 7 capsule did obviously not refer to a religious context. The technical object stood for the United States' unprecedented ability to equally control natural forces and a very complex human artifact like this one through science. Sending it around the world constituted the superiority of the United States nation, which was visibly able to design and build an object that could be sent into space and brought back unscathed at human will. This meaning got encapsulated in the aura of the object. The capsule had come back with material signs of its travel in outer space (scratches, burn marks), making the rocket into a national-sacred Real Presence and proof of the United States' outstanding potential in the present and for the future.

This superiority was particularly important against the background of the Cold War. In the 1960s and beyond, the Mercury Mission got staged as a signifier for a feeling of pride for the United States nation. Marc Jácome called this discourse the

---

30 Teasel Muir-Harmony, "Friendship 7's 'Fourth Orbit,'" *National Air and Space Museum,* February 16, 2012, https://airandspace.si.edu/stories/editorial/friendship-7%E2%80%99s-%E2%80%98fourth-orbit%E2%80%99.

31 The concept of Real Presence was coined by Marc Bloch, *Les Rois thaumaturges: Études sur le caractère surnaturel attribué à la puissance royale, particulièrement en France et en Angleterre* (Strasbourg: Librarie Istra, 1924). Ernst H. Kantorowicz, *The King's Two Bodies: A Study in Medieval Political Theology* (Princeton: Princeton University Press, 1957) elaborated the understanding that a king could act politically and theologically through a material double in funeral ceremonies. For a critical discussion which updates the concept to current research questions see Kristin Marek, *Die Körper des Königs: Effiges, Bildpolitik und Heiligkeit* (Munich: W. Fink, 2009).

narrative counterpart of the collective perception of Soviet successes as threat.[32]

Looking at the travelling capsule, the movement itself attracts attention, because it creates a narrative connection. Globally, the fourth orbit connected potential allies like pearls on a string of anti-communism. And also on a national level, the triumph of the space capsule might act in a unifying mission, since it travelled against the background of sweeping anti-communism and the violent battles over whiteness and race relations civil rights activists exposed and addressed. The Friendship 7 capsule came to its final halt in the "Milestones of Flight" gallery at the National Air and Space Museum on the national mall in Washington, DC, a signifying landscape "celebrating the country's democracy."[33] Today, the capsule's aura is still tangible for those who know and contribute to Friendship 7's message to unite, socially and politically.

Progress

In 2011, the Mercury Spacecraft MA-6 became one of the Institute of Electrical and Electronics Engineers (IEEE) milestones, a list of events designated as key historical achievements in electrical and electronic engineering. The electrical and electronic systems in this first US human-orbital flight on February 20, 1962 made, says the IEEE website, Glenn's "and future spaceflights possible."[34] Key contributions included the "navigation

32 Marc Jacome, "Remembering the Space Race: Nationalism and Heroic White America," *Academia.edu,* April 2013, https://www.academia. edu/6899237/Remembering_the_Space_Race_Nationalism_and_Heroic_ White_America.

33 Ari Shapiro and Maureen Pao, "Mission of African-American Museum Writ Large in Its Very Design," *WBUR News,* September 15, 2016, http:// www.wbur.org/npr/493909656/mission-of-african-american-museum- writ-large-in-its-very-design.

34 *Engineering and Technology History Wiki,* s.v. "Milestones:Mercury Space- craft MA-6, 1962," https://ethw.org/Milestones:Mercury_Spacecraft_MA- 6,_1962.

and control instruments, autopilot, rate stabilization and control, and fly-by-wire (FBW) systems."[35]

The explicit aim of the IEEE milestones is to celebrate feats of engineering excellence. The list produces not only nationalist celebrations (the first space flight with the Sputnik satellite, and the two preceding orbital flights, Vostok 1 with Yuri Gagarin and Vostok 2 with Gehrman Titov, have not been dedicated as IEEE milestones) but also broader expectations of progress. Progress, it is generally assumed, refers to engineering, technological, infrastructural, technical, scientific innovation. Progress is associated with forward or upward movement, with development, advancement, improvement, and superiority. It is associated with making the world better. It is more rarely associated with regress, with the social injustices facing, for instance, the Global South's factory workers, or with the environmental destruction caused by, for instance, digital rubbish.[36] The IEEE milestones sit alongside another IEEE program, REACH, "Raising Engineering Awareness through the Conduit of History." This program provides resources for social studies education which highlight the history of technologies and their impact on humanity. The single comment on the promotional video on YouTube refracts its core mission: "The message is that engineers throughout history have invented and built amazing machines that *help people.*"[37]

Through the historicizing of engineering, the Mercury spacecraft comes to signal hope in the possibility of helping people and making the world better. This fantasy of the good-life-to-come is tied up in a neoliberal agenda to convince students that careers in engineering are desirable *and also* in social, economic, and environmental inequalities *and also* in the messy

---

35 Ibid.

36 Jennifer Gabrys, *Digital Rubbish: A Natural History of Electronics* (Ann Arbor: University of Michigan Press, 2013).

37 engineeringhistory, "IEEE-REACH Promotional Video," *YouTube,* January 19, 2016, https://www.youtube.com/watch?v=5vmMxJrt3F4 (emphasis added).

dynamics of working towards "*social* progress,"[38] that is, in making the world a more just and equitable place, because if we are not invested in optimism, then how, asks Lauren Berlant, can life — in the ambivalent, uneven, precarious world of today — be made bearable?[39]

Space Race

The Space Race is an indispensable narrative element and metaphor for almost any account of the Cold War.[40] The same is true the other way around. To focus on one of the core material things in the Space Race — the rocket, the Friendship 7 — means to also "touch" another thing, the Vostok 1, the spacecraft that carried the Soviet Russian Yuri Gagarin and made him the first human in orbital space.[41] Through its mere material existence, Vostok 1 has the potential to decenter the US narrative of global progress and success. The Mercury Spacecraft MA-6 is made to mean differently if it is woven into a discursive web of things, which interrupts our writing and remembering from a standpoint of national or nationalistic historiography, from a Western, capitalist speaking position that "does" superiority.

Discursively speaking, the Friendship 7 was a tool to celebrate neutral, objective, scientific research and a specific concept of progress. The object participated in an ideological United States–Soviet, capitalist–communist war, in the mutual efforts to catch up and take over. However, semantically the Space Race metaphor covers over the military context of the Friendship 7. Materially, the Atlas rocket that launched Friendship 7 was "a modified ICBM (intercontinental ballistic missile) originally de-

38 Dietmar Dath and Barbara Kirchner, *Der Implex: Sozialer Fortschritt: Geschichte und Idee* (Berlin: Suhrkamp Verlag, 2012).

39 Lauren Gail Berlant, *Cruel Optimism* (Durham: Duke University Press, 2011), 14.

40 Silvia Berger Ziauddin, David Eugster, and Christa Wirth, eds. *Nach Feierabend 2017: Der kalte Krieg: Kältegrade eines globalen Konflikts* (Zürich: Diaphanes, 2017).

41 Haraway, *Companion Species Manifesto*, 98.

signed for nuclear warfare."[42] In fact, the San Diego Museum of Space describes the Atlas as the Unites States' first Intercontinental Ballistic Missile.[43] The spacecraft was a weapon.

Friendship 7 and the Atlas rocket thus are things that come to mean equivalently in a transnational narrative context just as in the national. Although centered on the United States, the spacecraft needs the Other to fully come to mean. There must be a shared materiality, and there is a shared narrative, the Space Race. The capsules, the men inside them, the tools and equipment, the technology and support around them, co-create the memories of what the Space Race was and is. In this ambivalence between progress, scientific excellence and victory (a "fair race" between competing scientists and engineers), and the weapon, tested vertically and threatening horizontally, is what the rocket in its referentiality represents. And this characteristic is mirrored in Vostok 1, as a *mise en abyme*.

Concluding words

This list is unfinished. We have accumulated seven items in a list of how the Friendship 7 capsule comes to mean. For some items, we have described material memory practices; for others, we have retold a history of the object. Material, stories, descriptions, historiography: each makes the past present in some way. Our goal was to open up the number of contexts we can give to any material thing. Our trope of the "and/also" re-emerges across the list. Why list these stories of the multiple ways that things hold together and touch one another? There is this list, as Haraway has written in *Staying with the Trouble,* "because there are quite definite response-abilities that are strengthened in such

---

42 "Atlas ICBM," *National Air and Space Museum,* June 14, 2016, https://airandspace.si.edu/stories/objects/mercury-friendship-7-atlas-icbm.

43 "Introduction," in *Atlas, America's First ICBM & Pioneering Workhorse of the U.S. Space Program, San Diego Air & Space Museum,* http://sandiegoairandspace.org/exhibits/online-exhibit-page/introduction2.

stories. The details matter."[44] The details link physical, material existences "to actual response-abilities." This quality links to Karen Barad's understanding of the material, "[t]he very nature of materiality is an entanglement. Matter itself is always already open to, rather entangled with, the 'Other.' The intra-actively emergent 'parts' of phenomena are coconstituted. [...] Ethics is therefore not about right response [sic] to a radically exterior/ized other, but about responsibility and accountability for the lively relationalities of becoming of which we are a part."[45]

As phallic body, scarred body, drugged body, white and black body, male and female body, interactive object, honoree, pioneer, adventurer, fun, behavior control, hashtag, craft beer, connected image, fuel supply, automation, colonial space, drama, real presence, American science and engineering, uniting element, fly-by-wire system, hope, ICBM, and, and, and, the Friendship 7 capsule, the Mercury 6 spacecraft and their human and more-than-human partners are making and remaking history, with the non-innocent ethical and political response-abilities which go along with these histories. "Why tell stories like my pigeon tales, when there are only more and more openings and no bottom lines?" asks Haraway.[46] Because stories strengthen response-abilities. Because the details matter.

There are observable tendencies to monopolize memory objects, to make them unambiguous. Multiple contextualizations poke holes in potentially very powerful singular memory narratives. We wanted to explore how things come to mean; our path there was to stutter, to add (and, and, and...) and to contextualize.

44 Donna J. Haraway, *Staying with the Trouble: Making Kin in the Chthulucene* (Durham: Duke University Press, 2016), 29.

45 Barad, *Meeting the Universe Halfway*, 393.

46 Haraway, *Staying with the Trouble*, 29.

Bibliography

"2017 International Air & Space Induction Celebration Set for Nov. 9." *San Diego Air & Space Museum,* 2017. http://sandiegoairandspace.org/blog/article/2017-international-air-space-induction-celebration-set-for-nov.-9.

Anderson, Elizabeth, Avril Maddrell, Kate McLoughlin, and Alana Vincent, eds. *Memory, Mourning, Landscape.* Amsterdam: Rodopi: 2010.

"Atlas ICBM." *National Air and Space Museum,* June 14, 2016. https://airandspace.si.edu/stories/objects/mercury-friendship-7-atlas-icbm.

Bal, Mieke. *Double Exposures: The Subject of Cultural Analysis.* New York: Routledge, 1996.

Barad, Karen. *Meeting the Universe Halfway: Quantum Physics and the Entanglement of Matter and Meaning.* Durham: Duke University Press, 2007.

———. "Posthumanist Performativity: Toward an Understanding of How Matter Comes to Matter." *Signs: Journal of Women in Culture and Society* 28, no. 3 (Spring 2003): 801–31. DOI: 10.1086/345321.

Berger Ziauddin, Silvia, David Eugster, and Christa Wirth, eds. *Nach Feierabend 2017: Der kalte Krieg: Kältegrade eines globalen Konflikts.* Zurich: Diaphanes, 2017.

Berlant, Lauren Gail. *Cruel Optimism.* Durham: Duke University Press, 2011.

"Be the Astronaut Opening in February." *San Diego Air & Space Museum,* 2017. http://sandiegoairandspace.org/newsletters/article/be-the-astronaut-opening-in-february.

Bloch, Marc. *Les Rois thaumaturges: Études sur le caractère surnaturel attribué à la puissance royale, particulièrement en France et en Angleterre.* Strasbourg: Librarie Istra, 1924.

Bowker, Geoffrey C. "All Knowledge Is Local." *Learning Communities* (2008): 138–49.

———. *Memory Practices in the Sciences.* Cambridge: MIT Press, 2008.

Campbell, Nancy. "Cold War Compulsions: U.S. Drug Science, Policy, and Culture." PhD diss., University of California at Santa Cruz, 1995.

Connerton, Paul. *How Societies Remember.* Cambridge: Cambridge University Press, 1995.

Dath, Dietmar, and Barbara Kirchner. *Der Implex: Sozialer Fortschritt: Geschichte und Idee.* Berlin: Suhrkamp Verlag, 2012.

Deleuze, Gilles, and Claire Parnet. *Dialogues II.* Translated by Hugh Tomlinson and Barbara Habberjam. London: Continuum, 2002.

engineeringhistory. "IEEE-REACH Promotional Video." *YouTube*, January 19, 2016. https://www.youtube.com/watch?v=5vmMxJrt3F4.

Gabrys, Jennifer. *Digital Rubbish: A Natural History of Electronics.* Ann Arbor: University of Michigan Press, 2013.

Gibson, Erin L.S. "Remembering Tomorrow: Wagon Roads, Identity and the Decolonization of a First Nations Landscape." *Public History Review* 23 (2016): 25–42. DOI: 10.5130/phrj.v23i0.5326.

Haraway, Donna J. *Companion Species Manifesto: Dogs, People, and Significant Otherness.* Chicago: Prickly Paradigm Press, 2003.

———. *Modest_Witness@Second_Millenium. FemaleMan.©Meets_OncoMouse™: Feminism and Technoscience.* New York: Routledge, 1997.

———. "Situated Knowledges: The Science Question in Feminism and the Privilege of Partial Perspective." *Feminist Studies* 14, no. 3 (Fall 1988): 575–99. DOI: 10.2307/3178066.

———. *Staying with the Trouble: Making Kin in the Chthulucene.* Durham: Duke University Press, 2016.

Hofsess, Brooke A., and Jennifer L. Sonenberg. "Enter: Ho/rhizoanalysis." *Cultural Studies ↔ Critical Methodologies* 13, no. 4 (2013): 299–308. DOI: 10.1177/1532708613487877.

Hoskins, Andrew. "Digital Network Memory." In *Mediation, Remediation, and the Dynamics of Cultural Memory,* edited by Astrid Erll and Ann Rigney, 91–106. Berlin: De Gruyter, 2009.

"Introduction." In *Atlas, America's First ICBM & Pioneering Workhorse of the U.S. Space Program, San Diego Air & Space Museum*. http://sandiegoairandspace.org/exhibits/online-exhibit-page/introduction2.

Ireland, Tracy, and Jane Lydon. "Rethinking Materiality, Memory and Identity." *Public History Review* 23 (2016): 1–8. DOI: 10.5130/phrj.v23i0.5333.

Jacome, Marc E. "Remembering the Space Race: Nationalism and Heroic White America." *Academia.edu,* April 2013. https://www.academia.edu/6899237/Remembering_the_Space_Race_Nationalism_and_Heroic_White_America.

Kanngieser, Anja. "… And … and … and … The Transversal Politics of Performative Encounters." *Deleuze Studies* 6, no. 2 (April 2012): 265–90. DOI: 10.3366/dls.2012.0062.

Kantorowicz, Ernst H. *The King's Two Bodies: A Study in Medieval Political Theology*. Princeton: Princeton University Press, 1957.

Law, John, Geir Afdal, Kristin Asdal, Wen-yuan Lin, Ingunn Moser, and Vicky Singleton. "Modes of Syncretism: Notes on Non-coherence." *CRESC Working Paper* 119 (2013).

Leigh Star, Susan, and James R. Griesemer. "Institutional Ecology, 'Translations' and Boundary Objects: Amateurs and Professionals in Berkeley's Museum of Vertebrate Zoology, 1907–39." *Social Studies of Science* 19, no. 3 (August 1989): 387–420. DOI: 10.1177/030631289019003001.

Marek, Kristin. *Die Körper des Königs: Effiges, Bildpolitik und Heiligkeit*. Munich: W. Fink, 2009.

Melfi, Theodore, dir. *Hidden Figures*. Los Angeles: 20th Century Fox, 2016.

Muir-Harmony, Teasel. "Friendship 7's 'Fourth Orbit.'" *Smithsonian National Air and Space Museum,* February 16, 2012. https://airandspace.si.edu/stories/editorial/friendship-7%E2%80%99s-%E2%80%98fourth-orbit%E2%80%99.

Rothberg, Michael. *Multidirectional Memory: Remembering the Holocaust in the Age of Decolonization.* Stanford: Stanford University Press, 2009.

Scott-Heron, Gil. "Whitey on the Moon." On *Small Talk at 125th and Lenox.* Ace Records Ltd, 1970. Vinyl disc. Available online at Ace Records, Ltd. "Gil Scott-Heron - Whitey On the Moon (Official Audio)." *YouTube,* August 19, 2014. https://www.youtube.com/watch?v=goh2x_G0ct4.

Shapiro, Ari, and Maureen Pao. "Mission of African-American Museum Writ Large in Its Very Design." *WBUR News,* September 15, 2016. http://www.wbur.org/npr/493909656/mission-of-african-american-museum-writ-large-in-its-very-design.

St. Pierre, Elizabeth A. "Post Qualitative Research: The Critique and the Coming After." In *The Sage Handbook of Qualitative Research,* edited by Norman K. Denzin and Yvonna S. Lincoln, 611–26. 4th edition. Los Angeles: Sage Publications, 2011.

van Dijck, José. "Flickr and the Culture of Connectivity: Sharing Views, Experiences, Memories." *Memory Studies* 4, no. 4 (October 2011): 401–15. DOI: 10.1177/1750698010385215.

Varutti, Marzia. "Polysemic Objects and Partial Translations: Museums and the Interpretation of Indigenous Material Culture in Taiwan." *Museum Anthropology* 37, no. 2 (September 2014): 102–17. DOI: 10.1111/muan.12056.

Verran, Helen. *Science and an African Logic.* Chicago: University of Chicago Press, 2001.

Williamson, Ben. "Decoding ClassDojo: Psycho-policy, Social-emotional Learning and Persuasive Educational Technologies." *Learning, Media and Technology* 42, no. 4 (January 2017): 440–53. DOI: 10.1080/17439884.2017.1278020.

3

Innocence

Lisa Farley

Innocence is a tricky construction. While signaling a state of happiness, moral purity, and "care-free enchantment," innocence is rife with conflict and linked to histories of social injustice.[1] The construction of innocence continues to orient a largely unquestioned educational idea: that children should be protected from the "difficult knowledge"[2] of the social and historical world as they become custodians of a better future.[3] At the core of this twin promise to redeem a broken world and be shielded from difficulty is, however, a racial paradox. The child figured in this fantasy is a presumed-to-be white child charged with the task of transforming the world from which they are also protected in the name of innocence.[4] Education is a hothouse for this paradox. With roots in Jean-Jacques Rousseau's idealized

1 Julie C. Garlen, "Interrogating Innocence: 'Childhood' as Exclusionary Social Practice," *Childhood* 26, no. 1 (February 2019): 55.

2 Deborah P. Britzman, *Lost Subjects, Contested Objects: Toward a Psychoanalytic Inquiry of Learning* (Albany: State University of New York Press, 1998), 118. "Difficult knowledge" refers both to the content on offer in curriculum and the psychical filters through which it is interpreted and often negated.

3 Madeleine R. Grumet, "The Lie of the Child Redeemer," *The Journal of Education* 168, no. 3 (October 1986): 89.

4 Fikile Nxumalo, *Decolonizing Place in Early Childhood Education* (New York: Routledge, 2019), 1.

fantasy of childhood as the embodiment of nature, schools continue uphold the dual aim to protect (white) children from historical violence even as they are constructed as little heroes sent to remake its troubling legacies anew.[5]

While much research in the area of history education has focused on representations in school textbooks and student and teacher interpretations of them, less attention has been given over to the idea of childhood as a historical artifact populating the imaginary of curriculum and pedagogy. In debates over what versions of history should be represented and how best to teach, questions about the "ideational and figurative force of [children's] existence" undergirding these arguments have been somewhat quiet.[6] In this chapter, I examine the force of innocence underlying the construction of the child as redeemer of the violent past. Although the promise of a better and brighter future is an alluring idea, particularly in the face of difficult knowledge, I suggest that the child redeemer is an ally to forgetting made from a melancholic wish to secure a fantasied time without conflict. I further suggest how the redeemer figure upholds unequal terrains of innocence between children and disavows those who are already born into history's painful legacies. The child redeemer functions to defend against the very past they are summoned to recuperate.

The Melancholy of Innocence and the Figure of the Child Redeemer

In "Mourning and Melancholia," Freud examines loss as the condition of humanity.[7] From the beginning, we are all subject to losses of both ordinary and extraordinary proportions.

---

5   Affrica Taylor, *Reconfiguring the Natures of Childhood* (New York, Routledge, 2013), 8.

6   Carolyn Steedman, *Strange Dislocations: Childhood and the Idea of Interiority 1750–1930* (Cambridge: Harvard University Press, 1995), 5.

7   Sigmund Freud, "Mourning and Melancholia," in *On Murder, Mourning and Melancholia,* ed. Adam Phillips, trans. Shaun Whiteside (London: Penguin Books, 2005), 201–32.

For Freud, two positions emerge in response to loss, and that are reflected in the title of his essay. Melancholia refers to an unconscious mode of identification that seeks to hold open a continuous engagement with loss in a bid to defend against the void it leaves behind.[8] Melancholia is painful, for in the effort to retain the lost other, the self takes the loss inside to the point of "devouring" its own center.[9] Mourning, by contrast, transforms the anguish of loss into memory, giving symbolic representation to the pain that melancholia holds tight. Freud acknowledges that melancholia and mourning are virtually indistinguishable. Both are marked by profound grief that takes shape in the withdrawal of attachments from the world in a protective gesture to prevent further pain. Together, melancholia and mourning represent a conflict: as we struggle to hold onto traces of lost others, we are also faced with the felt and undeniable presence of their absence.

One distinguishing feature of melancholia is, however, its unconscious ambivalence over loss, where "love and hatred struggle with one another."[10] Under the condition of melancholia, "the ego becomes split into absolute forms of good and bad that then wage for dominance."[11] The problem is that melancholic splitting is repressive, and, under its condition, the ego protects itself from encountering the conflictive qualities of grief. The split between love and hate becomes a self-enclosed deadlock that defends against "working through of the ambivalent feelings that accompany loss."[12] For instance, rather than confront feelings of hatred for having been abandoned to survive alone, the ego instead becomes "bound to the nostalgia for an ideal-

---

8   Ibid.

9   Ibid., 206.

10 Ibid., 216.

11 Deborah P. Britzman, "If the Story Cannot End: Deferred Action, Ambivalence, and Difficult Knowledge," in *Between Hope and Despair: Historical Trauma and Pedagogies of Remembrance,* eds. Roger I. Simon, Sharon Rosenberg, and Claudia Eppert (Lanham: Rowman & Littlefield, 2000), 34.

12 Ibid.

ized and unchanged world."[13] Ironically, the restorative effort of melancholia disavows the very loss it seeks to recover through the wish to return to an imaginary time before. The ego achieves this wish through the repetition of familiar dynamics that ward off any notice of the world as it has been changed because of the loss. Melancholia is, in this way, an unconscious project of self-mastery, for as Deborah Britzman writes, "what is actually idealized is not the object but the self."[14] That is, melancholia is a "narcissistic identification" that defends against the difficult work of acknowledging how loss undoes the ego's protective boundaries.[15] In Britzman's words, melancholia obstructs "an ethical struggle with reconstituting the self as subject to a relation that is no longer."[16] In the effort to recover the lost other, melancholia seeks to restore *the ego*'s lost sense of coherence.

The unconscious reach of melancholia also affects representations of historical loss in curriculum and pedagogy. Britzman, for one, finds traces of melancholia in controversies over the representation of *The Diary of Anne Frank*. In particular, Britzman unearths a melancholic tendency to idealize Anne Frank as a child beacon of hope that tempers questions of cultural genocide and sexuality that Frank also pens in her diary. Britzman identifies, too, how melancholia finds its way into uses of the diary that bolster a progressive educational narrative, made from a "pedagogical wish" that "if we can learn from another's pain we can avoid doing more harm."[17] While recognizing the importance of learning from historical trauma, Britzman reads the progressive quality of this narrative as a melancholic defense against "the dissonance that the difficulties of others can invoke."[18] For Madeleine Grumet, educational narratives of progress lean on the figure of the child redeemer, in whom adults invest the task of absolving a deeply injured world on the prom-

---

13 Ibid.
14 Ibid.
15 Ibid.
16 Ibid.
17 Ibid., 39.
18 Ibid.

ise of a future that does not have to suffer further devastation.[19] However, for both Britzman and Grumet, the wish that education — and the child — redeem the violent past is defensive. In the idealization of the child's education as the royal road to a future without conflict, there is a disavowal of the difficulties of facing trauma "that has already occurred"[20] and "the incommensurability of pain" that does not simply end.[21]

The redeemer is a melancholic figure that harbors ambivalence between, on the one hand, the wish to absolve historical violence, and on the other hand, the anxiety of children's fantasied loss of innocence in encountering representations of such violence. This ambivalence becomes split, leading to the idealization of the child and the disavowal of the historical violence that incited the wish for absolution in the first place. Cast in the logic of this split, the redeemer figure may also harbor a wish for no change at all. In the idealization of a future liberated from conflict, the child redeemer offers the promise of a world unaffected by loss, in Britzman's words, an "unchanged world."[22] Grumet points to a related irony that while adults impart children with the promise of change, they also tend to treat them as if they are not able to affect the world. And this is why, for Grumet, the child redeemer should be read as an "adorable symbol of society's self-deception, a means of foisting the mission of our own liberation on those least able to affect it."[23] Despite the idealization of the redeemer as change-agent, this little figure defends against that "ethical struggle," which, returning to Britzman, involves the ongoing labor of reconstituting the self in relation to a world as it has been, and continues to be, fundamentally altered by history's legacies.[24]

---

19 Grumet, "The Lie of the Child Redeemer," 91.
20 Britzman, "If the Story Cannot End," 42.
21 Ibid., 39.
22 Ibid., 34.
23 Grumet, "The Lie of the Child Redeemer," 89.
24 Britzman, "If the Story Cannot End," 34.

While "[t]eaching for social justice necessarily entails class-room discussions of inequity and injustice,"[25] debates about curriculum and pedagogy fall into the split logic of melancholia when the "good," usually attributed to "innocence," battles with the "bad" of difficult knowledge: trauma, state-sanctioned violence, and genocide. Deirdre M. Kelly and Mary Brooks find that teachers rely on this melancholic fracture when they invoke childhood innocence to explain their pedagogical choices to censor knowledge that they consider to be too "heavy."[26] These scholars observe, too, teachers' references to the related concept of "developmental appropriateness" that presumes an innocent child not yet capable of understanding.[27] Similarly, Julie E. Wollman-Bonilla finds that teachers "frequently argue that a text is inappropriate for children if the information or perspective(s) presented might, in their opinion, frighten children or introduce them to realities they don't or shouldn't know about."[28] At work in these discussions is a melancholic chasm between the good of childhood innocence and the bad of the world, where never the two shall meet.

Of course, arguments about what forms of representation count as appropriate are based not only on what adults "believe will appeal to children" but on what they believe "*should* appeal to them, or what they need to be taught."[29] As Perry Nodelman reminds us, adult perspectives are never neutral, but often telegraph the dominant cultural values of a given time and place. As it turns out, adults tend to want happy endings. In the context

---

25 Deirdre M. Kelly and Mary Brooks, "How Young Is Too Young? Exploring Beginning Teachers' Assumptions about Young Children and Teaching for Social Justice," *Equity and Excellence in Education* 42, no. 2 (2009): 204.

26 Ibid., 208.

27 Ibid., 209. See also Jonathan G. Silin, *Sex, Death, and the Education of Children: Our Passion for Ignorance in the Age of AIDS* (New York: Teachers College Press, 1995), 81–110.

28 Julie E. Wollman-Bonilla, "Outrageous Viewpoints: Teachers' Criteria for Rejecting Works of Children's Literature," *Language Arts* 75, no. 4 (April 1998): 289–90.

29 Perry Nodelman, *The Hidden Adult: Defining Children's Literature* (Baltimore: John Hopkins University Press, 2008), 5 (emphasis added).

of early childhood education, Sandra Chang-Kredl and Gala Wilkie suggest that this tendency serves an emotional function. They propose that teachers choose to read what they perceive as happy narratives with a nostalgic view to recuperate a good version of their own childhood.[30] Drawing from Grumet, Chang-Kredl and Wilkie speculate that adults read children's books as "portals to childhood, inviting us to 'recuperate our losses,' to reconcile with the parts from which we have been separated."[31] The lost parts that teachers seek out are, more often than not, "constructions of the child as innocent, joyful and free."[32] That adults prefer the happily-ever-after aesthetic of children's books supports Wollman-Bonilla's observation that teachers tend to censor traumatic literature based on its "failure to represent what they see as dominant social values."[33] This is true, Wollman-Bonilla suggests, even when such values are recognized as "myths" that in fact reinstall normative ways of being.[34]

This proclivity to procure positive affect and protect childhood innocence, however, risks silencing children's embodied experiences of living in a world of social and historical conflict. What is more, such efforts disappear children's agency, casting them in terms of "inadequacy and dependency."[35] In turn, this lowly position props up the related idea of progress linked to colonial domination and that represents, in Grumet's words, "patriarchy manipulating its young in order to sustain its own power, control, and privilege."[36] So long as children are innocent, they secure the adult's desire for power, symbolizing, in Jacqueline Rose's words, "just how far we've come."[37] In this

---

30 Sandra Chang-Kredl and Gala Wilkie, "What Is It Like to Be a Child? Childhood Subjectivity and Teacher Memories as Heterotopia," *Curriculum Inquiry* 46, no. 3 (2016): 309.

31 Ibid., 309–10.

32 Ibid., 315.

33 Wollman-Bonilla, "Outrageous Viewpoints," 290.

34 Ibid.

35 Grumet, "The Lie of the Child Redeemer," 89.

36 Ibid.

37 Rose, *The Case of Peter Pan*, 13.

context of unequal power, Jonathan G. Silin suggests that when teachers invoke innocence or developmental readiness to explain why they do not engage children in discussions of difficult knowledge, they may be protecting themselves from their own sense of vulnerability.[38] Pedagogical practices and representations that deny, omit, or gloss over conditions of past violence not only fail children, but also history itself.[39] The question is, here, whether teachers may "worry *too little* about the possibility of muting the moral gravity and complexity of genocide through well-intentioned emphases on rescuing and salvation," often mobilized in the name of childhood innocence.[40]

The cementing of childhood and innocence underlying these discussions of representation and education has its own history. In her analysis of the US context, Julie C. Garlen notes that the concept of innocence "began to take hold" to secure the privileges and protections of white children in a time of social and economic change, when industrialization, immigration, and abolition "threatened to destabilize the white patriarchal political structure."[41] For racially minoritized children, however, this classification of childhood calcified into a discourse of infantilization justifying violent interventions in the name of progress.[42] For instance, innocence bolstered a logic of racial inferiority used to justify the forced removal of Indigenous children from their homes and into Residential Schools presuming to provide "'appropriate' conditions of childhood."[43] Thus while childhood

---

38 Silin, *Sex, Death, and the Education of Children,* 51.

39 For a discussion of the ways that children's and young adult literature evades social and historical violence, see Jane M. Gangi, *Genocide in Contemporary Children's and Young Adult Literature: Cambodia to Darfur* (New York: Routledge, 2014).

40 Robertson, *Teaching for a Tolerant World,* 5 (emphasis added).

41 Garlen, "Interrogating Innocence," 60.

42 Erica R. Meiners, *For the Children? Protecting Innocence in a Carceral State* (Minneapolis: University of Minnesota Press, 2016). See also Robin Bernstein, *Racial Innocence: Performing American Childhood from Slavery to Civil Rights* (New York: New York University Press, 2011).

43 Garlen, "Interrogating Innocence," 63. See also Joanne Faulkner, *The Importance of Being Innocent: Why We Worry about Children* (Cambridge:

innocence was a protection for white children, it was a colonial tool of dehumanization for others.[44] At stake in debates about whether a text is "developmentally appropriate" is not simply, then, an individual child's cognitive and emotional readiness to encounter difficulty, but a highly privileged and paternalistic concept of childhood used to nurture legacies that exclude minoritized children from its limited imagination. "Childhood," in the words of Erica R. Meiners "has historically never been available to all."[45]

If education is to be meaningful, what is required is a more nuanced conceptualization of childhood than can be imagined through the melancholic filter of innocence.[46] As Gareth Matthews argued over two decades ago, children's capacities are too often under-estimated in relationship to knowledge that is perceived to be difficult or complex.[47] Concerns about developmental readiness — or unreadiness as the case may be — are melancholic insofar as they are carried on a wish to return to an idealized time of childhood innocence that secures a fantasy of the adult in charge, where neither extreme actually exists. In listening to children themselves, however, the modern adult/child binary crumbles. Judith P. Robertson, for one, notes how

Cambridge University Press, 2011).

44 Toby Rollo, "Feral Children: Settler Colonialism, Progress, and the Figure of the Child," *Settler Colonial Studies* 8, no. 1 (2018): 71.

45 Meiners, *For the Children?*, 6.

46 For more on the debates about trauma texts, education, and constructions of childhood, see Lisa Farley, *Childhood Beyond Pathology: A Psychoanalytic Study of Development and Diagnosis* (Albany: State University of New York Press, 2018); Gangi, *Genocide in Contemporary Children's and Young Adult Literature*; Kelly and Brooks, "How Young Is Too Young?"; Kenneth B. Kidd, "'A' is for Auschwitz: Psychoanalysis, Trauma Theory, and the 'Children's Literature of Atrocity,'" *Children's Literature* 33 (2005): 120–49; Susan Lehr, ed., *Battling Dragons: Issues and Controversies in Children's Literature* (Portsmouth: Heinemann, 1995); Judith P. Robertson, ed., *Teaching for a Tolerant World Grades K–6: Essays and Resources* (Urbana: National Council of Teachers of English, 1999); and Silin, *Sex, Death, and the Education of Children.*

47 Gareth B. Matthews, *The Philosophy of Childhood* (Cambridge: Harvard University Press, 1996).

the "spontaneous curiosity" of children's questions sets into motion a chronicle of conflicts that "provoke in adults a jumbled hansard of emotion that feels like anything but mature or self-assured response."[48] If the figure of the child redeemer resurrects a fantasied position of the adult's certainty, then Robertson reminds us that children's questions activate the adult's vulnerability, provided we can bear this feeling. The challenge is how adults, including teachers, can mourn the construct of innocence and confront the conflicts, uncertainties, and questions that difficult knowledge churns up not only in children, but in themselves.

The Honesty of the Daughter's Lies

Despite the questions that educational theorists, teachers, and children themselves raise about difficult knowledge, censorship abounds. In the North American context, we can find evidence of this appetite for exclusion in the American Library Association's (ALA) annually published lists of "challenged books," which document requests put forth by administrators, librarians, teachers, parents, and/or community members seeking the removal of a text from school and public libraries, reading lists, and curricula. Compiled by the Office of Intellectual Freedom, the aim of the ALA's lists is to promote awareness about censorship, noting on its website that "85 percent of actual challenges to library materials receive no media attention and remain unreported."[49] Among challenged books are both young adult and adult texts but, as the ALA reports, "[f]requently, challenges are motivated by the desire to protect children."[50] Here, I would specify the desire to protect the construction of childhood innocence. Indeed, a good number of challenged books represent issues of historical trauma, sexuality, marginalization, and racism

---

48 Robertson, Teaching for a Tolerant World, 5.

49 Robert P. Doyle, "Books Challenged or Banned 2014–2015," *American Library Association,* March 2015, 3.

50 Ibid.

that pierce the borders of this precious fantasy.[51] Of these, and significant to my previous discussion, *The Diary of Anne Frank* is included on the ALA's list of "frequently challenged books with diverse content," where challenges cite Frank's references to death camps and her own maturing sexuality.[52]

One of the most "frequently challenged" books on this same list is another diary, Sherman Alexie's young adult fiction, *The Absolutely True Diary of a Part-time Indian*.[53] The narrative tells the story of fourteen-year-old Junior Spirit who lives with his family on the homeland referred to in the book as the Spokane Indian Reservation, located near Wellpinit in Washington state. Throughout, Junior struggles with the question of what it can mean to carve out a meaningful relationship to his education in the wake of the Residential School, the very institution used in the colonial aim of cultural genocide. When Junior decides to leave the reservation to enroll in a high school predominantly attended by white students, he faces a number of conflicts. Although he excels on the basketball team, makes new friends, and develops his first crush, Junior is also subject to the anti-Indigenous racism of the school curriculum, the team mascot, teachers, and the very same people who claim to be his friends. Despite these conflicts, David Lewkowich finds that new teachers tend to idealize Junior's upward climb through schooling. Over and over, they insist that Junior represents the "promise of success and salvation through education."[54] However, Lewkowich suggests that the construction of Junior as an idealized pedagogical subject actually idealizes the role of the teacher in the face of difficult knowledge, confirming, as he writes, "the fantasy

51 "Defining Diversity," *American Library Association,* March 2016, http://www.ala.org/advocacy/bbooks/diversity.

52 "Frequently Challenged Books with Diverse Content," *American Library Association,* August, 2016, http://www.ala.org/advocacy/bbooks/frequent-lychallengedbooks/diverse.

53 Sherman Alexie, *The Absolutely True Diary of a Part-time Indian* (New York: Little, Brown & Company, 2007).

54 David Lewkowich, "Transference of Teacher-casting and Projections of Redemption: Teacher Education, Young Adult Literature and the Psychic Life of Reading," *Pedagogy, Culture & Society* 23, no. 3 (2015): 360.

of teaching as a job whose meaning is discernible, measurable, and certain."[55] The idealization of Junior not only works to rescue the teacher's sense of self-mastery, it also defends against the more difficult question of what it can mean to enter into a profession that is mired in ongoing legacies of social violence.

Cast in the language of melancholia, redemptive readings of Junior produce a split between his "success and salvation" and the conflicts he also represents.[56] At the core of these is a tension between, on the one hand, Junior's inheritance of colonial legacies pressing down on his life chances, and on the other hand, his efforts "to continue becoming in new and unexpected ways" in spite of this inheritance.[57] Unlike the stereotype of the child redeemer, Junior's efforts to work through this tension are not individually heroic; they are entangled in social structures and power relations that reproduce anti-Indigenous racism, cycles of poverty, addiction, and social violence. Challenges to Alexie's book name precisely these issues as reason for its censorship. Sexuality is also cited in objections to the book's inclusion in curriculum and reading lists. For instance, as reported by the ALA, parents in Meridian, Idaho complained that Alexie's novel "discusses masturbation, contains profanity, and has been viewed as anti-Christian."[58] Further to this, the book was challenged at the Cedar Grove Middle School in Washington on the ground that, "the book contains numerous depictions of sexual behavior, as well as instances of racism, vulgar language, bullying and violence."[59] If, as observed above, Junior is read as a child redeemer, then as importantly, he also transgresses the myth of innocence typically pinned to this figure.

We read Alexie's novel in a course I teach on the history of education in the Faculty of Education where I work in Toronto, Canada. When I ask the beginning teachers of my classes

---

55 Ibid., 364.

56 Ibid., 360.

57 RM Kennedy, "Toward a Cosmopolitan Curriculum of Forgiveness," *Curriculum Inquiry* 41 no. 3 (2011): 383.

58 Doyle, "Books Challenged or Banned 2014–2015," 4.

59 Ibid.

whether they would include Alexie's novel in their curriculum, they communicate a melancholic split. On the one hand, they articulate, with some guilt, their own love of the novel, including Alexie's bawdy references and his bold representation of difficult emotions: shame, anger, loneliness, and sadness. They also express a hope that they might one day teach Alexie's book as part of their overall efforts to redress the impacts of colonial history. On the other hand, they just ask quickly conjure an innocent child, citing the very concerns that are reported to the ALA. Many beginning teachers speculate that the younger the child reader, the more likely they will be negatively influenced by Alexie's depictions of bullying and enticed to borrow from his characters' uses of profanity. Still others worry about Junior's references to sexuality, masturbation, and one very funny conversation with his friend Gordy, who admits that books give him a "boner."[60] If only Alexie hadn't included those sexual references, they assert.

Despite their enjoyment of Alexie's book and their considerations of its pedagogical value, the new teachers of my classrooms ultimately assume and worry about an innocent child reader that puts a halt on further discussion about the work of social transformation through education. And, while their expressed anxieties about Alexie's depictions of sexuality may seem to have little to do with history, these concerns may be read as affective traces of colonialism authorizing which forms of sexual expression and versions of childhood are appropriate (i.e., innocent) and those that are not. However, as discussed above, the construct of innocence is not itself innocent; it is an effect of colonial history guarding the borders of childhood as the "exclusive property of whiteness" that sets the terms for who gets to have a childhood at all.[61] When the child redeemer is conjured in response to the violent past, what is also conjured is a very particular notion of childhood that, returning to Meiners, has never included all children.

---

60 Alexie, *The Absolutely True Diary of a Part-time Indian*, 96.
61 Garlen, "Interrogating Innocence," 61.

In light of these "asymmetries of innocence,"[62] it is significant that Grumet offers a second child figure, the child redeemer's sister, who she strikingly refers to as the lying daughter.[63] For Grumet, the lying daughter is not simply a naughty child needing correction, even while it may be tempting to read her this way. Rather, this child figure offers a critical commentary on the "contrivance" of innocence by exposing the conflicted quality of our ties to the historical world.[64] As Grumet puts it, the daughter's lie "represents a chosen separation, a willful withdrawal from the adult world" and, in this way, refuses to repeat inherited legacies.[65] It is not "the son's innocence" but in "the daughter's lies" where hope resides for, in Grumet's words, "fibs and stories speak another way of knowing and being in the world, one that runs under the symbols of conventional knowledge and discourse."[66] Where the child redeemer implies a melancholic escape hatch from the violent past, the lying daughter encodes the entangled qualities of historical relationships that, under the guise of innocence, we might be "afraid to remember or imagine."[67] She offers a frank representation of the complex and painful terms of growing up amid legacies of colonial violence and so upsets the progressive fantasy of the innocent child marching seamlessly toward a happy and bright future. Conflict, not heroic redemption, is her emotional situation.

Alexie includes a lying daughter in his novel. Mary Runs Away is Junior's older sister who he describes as "beautiful and

---

62 I borrow the term, "asymmetries of innocence" from the title of Hannah Dyer's book, *The Queer Aesthetics of Childhood: Asymmetries of Innocence and the Cultural Politics of Child Development* (New Brunswick: Rutgers University Press, 2019). In this work, Dyer draws from literature and film to show how colonial scripts of innocence harm children when they deny and disappear the gendered, classed, and racialized intersections of existence.

63 Grumet, "The Lie of the Child Redeemer," 91.

64 Ibid.

65 Ibid.

66 Ibid., 95.

67 Ibid.

strong and funny."[68] As her name suggests, Mary Runs Away regularly runs away from home. Disillusioned, Mary Runs Away one last time, gets married, and moves to St. Ignatius in Montana. Tragically, she and her new husband are killed when their recreational vehicle (RV) trailer burns to the ground. Her family, friends, and community are devastated. Thinking with Grumet's construction, Mary Runs Away may be read as a "lying daughter" who lifts the veil on the lie of romanticizing the child redeemer of a troubled world. Alexie hints at precisely this illusion with a literary inflection: Mary Runs Away wanted to "write romance novels" but never did.[69] Mary Runs Away's thwarted desire is not her individual failure, but symbolizes the failure of Western culture's romance with childhood innocence. The death of Mary Runs Away charges education with a responsibility to invite children and young people to claim their chosen separation — their willful withdrawal — from legacies seeking to control, and ultimately arrest, their movement. She raises a question of how teachers may support young people to make meaningful connections to the world in ways that refuse to condemn them to fated scripts: that is, to author "altered accounts" of the legacies they inherit.[70] It is not enough, however, to uphold Mary Runs Away as a better alternative to the construction of innocence. To take this position, particularly from a settler point of view, is to risk idealizing children's pain and pathologizing entire generations as doomed.[71] Mary Runs Away rather bequeaths to teachers a challenge to support young people to create viable paths that depart from set channels of history and to re-signify a relationship to its legacies. Without having to die for it.

Admittedly, lying is difficult knowledge carrying troubling connotations, particularly in the context of history education.

---

68 Alexie, *The Absolutely True Diary of a Part-time Indian*, 28.

69 Ibid., 40.

70 Grumet, "The Lie of the Child Redeemer," 95.

71 Krista Maxwell, "Historicizing Historical Trauma Theory: Troubling the Trans-generational Transmission Paradigm," *Transcultural Psychiatry* 51, no. 3 (June 2014): 412.

As it signifies in this chapter, however, the figure of the lying daughter unearths hard truths that the innocent son defends against. In the lying daughter are laid bare ongoing legacies of colonialism impacting children's experiences and that are implicated in their uneven recognition *as* children within a frame of innocence. "Not buried in nostalgia or paranoia," the lying daughter is a storyteller who publishes the contradictory realities of both childhood and history.[72] While schools are "designed to seclude innocent sons" — protecting them from the world they are expected to heroically transform — the lying daughter offers a frank representation of the difficulties of trying to carve out a place for the self in the long shadows of history.[73] She tells a story about what it can mean to walk away from colonial legacies while recognizing the impossibility of absolving their implication in reproducing drastic inequities between children. She tells a story of revolt against the white privilege of innocence and the dehumanization of all those cast outside of its borders. Indeed, she tells a story about how innocence is itself a lie and why it is time to speak honestly about the need to let go of this highly divisive and worn-out construct.

Mourning Innocence

Now is the time for education to confront and work through the figurative force of childhood populating discussions of curriculum and pedagogy. One such force is the child redeemer that opens onto two sides of a melancholic wish: to rescue the world from the violent past and to protect (white) children from the pain of this encounter. What the redeemer figure actually protects is the privileged ideal of childhood innocence that, returning to Garlen, "has operated to maintain White supremacy" and refuses to account for the ways in which children are always already — and unequally — affected by the violence of colonial

---

72 Grumet, "The Lie of the Child Redeemer," 95.
73 Ibid.

legacies.[74] What remains is a question about how teachers and theorists can mourn the fantasied innocence of the child sent to redeem education from its implication in the violent past and challenge the structures of inequity upheld by this exhausting figure. It may be time, citing Grumet once more, "to turn to the unsung sisters" of "cherubic boys" in order to account for and redress the many injustices that are the ground of education, and to reimagine the work of teaching and learning anew.[75]

In relation to this last point, Teresa Strong-Wilson, Amarou Yoder, and Christina Phipps emphasize the value of pedagogical practices that engage questions of social (in)justice over innocence. They find that teachers who teach with trauma texts are "pushing the boundaries" about what we think we know about children and the communities in which they live.[76] Pedagogical practices that engage difficult knowledge are "unsettling," these scholars suggest, because they invite both teachers and children to account for the ongoing impacts of colonial legacies affecting understandings about education, childhood, and existence itself.[77] Arguably, boundary-pushing teachers also make a willful departure from the construct of innocence that has and continues to define which children are thought to belong to the very category of childhood. In so doing, they welcome a more complex view of children as touched by difficult knowledge while at the same time refusing individualizing narratives of either inadequacy or redemption. When we can loosen up on the idealization of childhood innocence, and when we can acknowledge that *that* idealization is a melancholic tool upholding race privilege and historical denial, then education might become a site in which to confront the world as it exists in all its violence, conflict, and failure. This insight is not the end of education but

---

74 Garlen, "Interrogating Innocence," 56.

75 Grumet, "The Lie of the Child Redeemer," 91.

76 Teresa Strong-Wilson, Amarou Yoder, and Heather Phipps, "Going Down the Rabbit Hole: Teachers' Engagements with 'Dialectical Images' in Canadian Children's Literature on Social Justice," *Changing English: Studies in Culture and Education* 21, no. 1 (2014): 88.

77 Ibid., 87.

rather marks the end of a melancholic education and the beginning of learning from history's discontents.

Bibliography

Alexie, Sherman. *The Absolutely True Diary of a Part-time Indian.* New York: Little, Brown & Company, 2007.

Bernstein, Robin. *Racial Innocence: Performing American Childhood from Slavery to Civil Rights.* New York: New York University Press, 2011.

Britzman, Deborah P. "If the Story Cannot End: Deferred Action, Ambivalence, and Difficult Knowledge." In *Between Hope and Despair: Historical Trauma and Pedagogies of Remembrance,* edited by Roger I. Simon, Sharon Rosenberg, and Claudia Eppert, 27–57. Lanham: Rowman & Littlefield, 2000.

———. *Lost Subjects, Contested Objects: Toward a Psychoanalytic Inquiry of Learning.* Albany: State University of New York Press, 1998.

Chang-Kredl, Sandra, and Gala Wilkie. "What Is It Like to Be a Child? Childhood Subjectivity and Teacher Memories as Heterotopia." *Curriculum Inquiry* 46, no. 3 (2016): 308–20. DOI: 10.1080/03626784.2016.1168262.

"Defining Diversity." *American Library Association,* March 2016. http://www.ala.org/advocacy/bbooks/diversity.

Doyle, Robert P. "Books Challenged or Banned 2014–2015." *American Library Association,* March 2015. http://hdl.handle.net/11213/8176.

Dyer, Hannah. *The Queer Aesthetics of Childhood: Asymmetries of Innocence and the Cultural Politics of Child Development.* New Brunswick: Rutgers University Press, 2019.

Farley, Lisa. *Childhood Beyond Pathology: A Psychoanalytic Study of Development and Diagnosis.* Albany: State University of New York Press, 2018.

Faulkner, Joanne. *The Importance of Being Innocent: Why We Worry about Children.* Cambridge: Cambridge University Press, 2011.

"Frequently Challenged Books with Diverse Content," *American Library Association,* August, 2016. http://www.ala.org/advocacy/bbooks/frequentlychallengedbooks/diverse.

Freud, Sigmund. "Mourning and Melancholia." In *On Murder, Mourning and Melancholia,* edited by Adam Phillips. Translated by Shaun Whiteside, 201–32. London: Penguin Books, 2005.

Gangi, Jane M. *Genocide in Contemporary Children's and Young Adult Literature: Cambodia to Darfur.* New York: Routledge, 2014.

Garlen, Julie C. "Interrogating Innocence: 'Childhood' as Exclusionary Social Practice." *Childhood* 26, no. 1 (February 2019): 54–67. DOI: 10.1177/0907568218811484.

Griffith, Jane. *Words Have a Past: The English Language, Colonialism, and the Newspapers of Indian Boarding Schools.* Toronto: University of Toronto Press, 2019.

Grumet, Madeleine R. "The Lie of the Child Redeemer." *The Journal of Education* 168, no. 3 (October 1986): 87–97. DOI: 10.1177/002205748616800310.

Kelly, Deirdre M., and Mary Brooks. "How Young Is Too Young? Exploring Beginning Teachers' Assumptions about Young Children and Teaching for Social Justice." *Equity and Excellence in Education* 42, no. 2 (2009): 202–16. DOI: 10.1080/10665680902739683.

Kennedy, RM. "Toward a Cosmopolitan Curriculum of Forgiveness." *Curriculum Inquiry* 41 no. 3 (2011): 373–93. DOI: 10.1111/j.1467-873X.2011.00551.x.

Kidd, Kenneth B. "'A' is for Auschwitz: Psychoanalysis, Trauma Theory, and the 'Children's Literature of Atrocity'." *Children's Literature* 33 (2005): 120–49. DOI: 10.1353/chl.2005.0014.

Lehr, Susan, ed. *Battling Dragons: Issues and Controversies in Children's Literature.* Portsmouth: Heinemann, 1995.

Lewkowich, David. "Transference of Teacher-casting and Projections of Redemption: Teacher Education, Young Adult Literature and the Psychic Life of Reading." *Pedagogy, Culture & Society* 23, no. 3 (2015): 349–68. DOI: 10.1080/14681366.2014.977808.

Matthews, Gareth B. *The Philosophy of Childhood.* Cambridge: Harvard University Press, 1996.

Maxwell, Krista. "Historicizing Historical Trauma Theory: Troubling the Trans-generational Transmission Paradigm." *Transcultural Psychiatry* 51, no. 3 (June 2014): 407–35. DOI: 10.1177/1363461514531317.

Meiners, Erica R. *For the Children? Protecting Innocence in a Carceral State.* Minneapolis: University of Minnesota Press, 2016.

Nodelman, Perry. *The Hidden Adult: Defining Children's Literature.* Baltimore: John Hopkins University Press, 2008.

Nxumalo, Fikile. *Decolonizing Place in Early Childhood Education.* New York: Routledge, 2019.

Robertson, Judith P., ed. *Teaching for a Tolerant World Grades K–6: Essays and Resources.* Urbana: National Council of Teachers of English, 1999.

Rollo, Toby. "Feral Children: Settler Colonialism, Progress, and the Figure of the Child." *Settler Colonial Studies* 8, no. 1 (2018): 60–79. DOI: 10.1080/2201473X.2016.1199826

Rose, Jaqueline. *The Case of Peter Pan: Or, the Impossibility of Children's Literature.* Philadelphia: University of Pennsylvania Press, 1992.

Silin, Jonathan G. *Sex, Death, and the Education of Children: Our Passion for Ignorance in the Age of AIDS.* New York: Teachers College Press, 1995.

Steedman, Carolyn. *Strange Dislocations: Childhood and the Idea of Interiority 1750–1930.* Cambridge: Harvard University Press, 1995.

Strong-Wilson, Teresa, Amarou Yoder, and Heather Phipps. "Going Down the Rabbit Hole: Teachers' Engagements with 'Dialectical Images' in Canadian Children's Literature on Social Justice." *Changing English: Studies in Culture and Education* 21, no. 1 (2014): 79–93. DOI: 10.1080/1358684X.2013.876143.

Wollman-Bonilla, Julie E. "Outrageous Viewpoints: Teachers' Criteria for Rejecting Works of Children's Literature." *Language Arts* 75, no. 4 (April 1998): 287–95.

4

Responsibility

Matthew Howard

Responsibility and memory are indelibly linked. From the banal encouragement of one person to another to "remember the passports" before setting off on a holiday to the more profound "lest we forget" associated with national commemorations of fallen service people, there is a clear sense that obligation and recollection are tied together. However, this chapter is situated within a book encouraging the exploration of the limits of memory. In this respect, I am invited to explore what responsibilities lie at the limits of memory. There is, for instance, a forgetting closely associated with remembering.[1] What, and who, is forgotten? What is enacted in and by memory's limitations?

In addition to exploring why a sense of obligation and memory are so closely bound together, it is also important to explore the processes by which memories are made intelligible as memories at all. How are certain mnemonic narratives given normative and formative power while other more critical,

---

1   On the entanglement between remembering and forgetting, see, for example, John Shotter, "The Social Construction of Remembering and Forgetting," in *Collective Remembering*, eds. David Middleton and Derek Edwards (London: Sage Publications, 1990), 120–38; Paul Connerton, *How Modernity Forgets* (Cambridge: Cambridge University Press, 2009).

equivocal, or oppositional narratives are cast aside?[2] The focus of this chapter, then, is not on responsibility associated with memory itself but the academic responsibility to position oneself in a way which enables the exploration of the mechanics of memory. The importance of this sense of responsibility toward memory as discipline, as far as my own research goes, is built on Shaunnagh Dorsett and Shaun McVeigh's notion of responsibility. In the context of defining jurisdiction, they establish that responsibility is an important characteristic of "holding office."[3] By extension, the holding of office can be reimagined in an academic context. Here, office relates to that of the student within an academic community who is obligated, among other things, to commit to critical research. Alongside this idea of responsibility sits an affinity to materiality-inflected methodologies that seek to trace the manner by which things come to be enacted. Such methodologies extend the participative roles in such enactments to a variety of things. Conflating this methodological positioning with the aforementioned ethical notion of responsibility brings up the notion of having responsibility to explore and reveal the detail of how things, more specifically memories, come to be constructed. Section one briefly sets out how this approach is suited to the study of the elements which constitute memory, particularly in relation to the critical potential it offers when considering questions of mnemonic and historical "truth."

This chapter seeks to exemplify this point in relation to the commemoration of Anzac Day (a day of remembrance in Australia and New Zealand originating from the involvement of the Australian and New Zealand Army Corps in World War I) and the reverence of C.E.W. Bean's accounts, and other writings from the soldiers themselves, of the Australian presence in World War I. In focusing on a single element of the Anzac

---

2   For more on the exploration of the formative and normative power of memory, see Jan Assmann, *Cultural Memory and Early Civilization: Writing, Remembrance, and Political Imagination* (Cambridge: Cambridge University Press, 2011).

3   Shaunnagh McVeigh and Shaun Dorsett, *Jurisdiction* (London: Routledge, 2012), 24ff

Day commemorative pattern (i.e., written artifacts), a space is opened up for the articulation of the role it might play in the enactment of a mnemonic narrative. It also offers the opportunity for acknowledging what is invoked in order to make a feature of a commemorative narrative so persuasive and, consequentially, what this says about memory formation.

Section two serves to demonstrate that Bean's account is a factor in the formation of the Anzac commemorative narrative. It also seeks to question this narrative: what work has gone into creating it? What work has gone into arrogating the position of this particular recollection over others? It particularly seeks to implicate the distribution and regularity of film and televisual representations of Bean's authority and a particular Anzac narrative. It suggests that historical and mnemonic authority is performed. The final section of this chapter briefly considers what the performativity of memory says about duties and responsibilities tied to memory. It suggests that the importance of addressing the question of memory's character, by acknowledging the lack of authority or authenticity in truth, can be cast on both social and political bases on the one hand and an ethical basis on the other.

The Performativity of Memory and Critical Responsibility

One aspect of attending responsibly to the discipline of memory studies is establishing exactly what is being studied and how. For instance, since Maurice Halbwachs advanced a definition of memories as a collective phenomenon,[4] contingent on sociality, a rift between individualist and collectivist perspectives has developed within the study of memory.[5] Lost in the debate about whether memory is the prerogative of the individual or inherently and necessarily social is an attentiveness towards the con-

---

4   Maurice Halbwachs, *On Collective Memory*, ed. and trans. Lewis A. Coser (Chicago: University of Chicago Press, 1992).

5   Jeffrey K. Olick, "Collective Memory: The Two Cultures," *Sociological Theory* 17, no. 3 (1999): 333–48.

ditioning of memory beyond the human. Students of collective memory studies, whether individualist or collectivist, can fall into the trap of eliding the non-human entities that are invoked and deployed in the enactment of a mnemonic narrative.

The collectivist perspective can, perhaps, more readily apprehend how memory is socialized and situated beyond the human, given their insistence on memory as a product of sociality. However, a greater insistence on the non-human actors in memory is required when exploring the character of memory.[6] To this end, understanding "social" to mean the association of radically symmetrical actors, whether human or not, allows us to rethink memory and address how it is proliferated.[7] Indeed, Andrew Hoskins makes a similar appeal by suggesting we should talk about *connective* rather than *collective* memory.[8] This more fittingly characterizes memory as a relationally enacted thing, contingent on environmental factors.

The reason it is important to move beyond the simple individualist-collectivist dichotomy is that it invites us to challenge the foundations on which memories come to be built and characterized. For instance, a recognition of the materiality or ecology of memory is a recognition that moves it beyond the inviolability of psychologism or, at best, the threshold truths which are fleshed out discursively. Instead, it asks us to consider the form and capacity a memory takes on as being a product of the choreography, ordering, and relationality of a number of diffuse elements.

Opening up the exploration of memory institutions to these diffuse elements, such as "the proliferation of the archive via

---

6   Alan Radley, "Artefacts, Memory, and a Sense of the Past," in *Collective Remembering,* eds. David Middleton and Derek Edwards (London: Sage Publications, 1990), 46–59.

7   For a reimagined definition of the social, more inclusive of a variety of non-human actors, too, see Bruno Latour, *Reassembling the Social: An Introduction to Actor-Network-Theory* (Oxford: Oxford University Press, 2005).

8   Andrew Hoskins, "Memory Ecologies," *Memory Studies* 9, no. 3 (2016): 348–57.

digitization" is important because, continuing with the example of the archive, it demonstrates that the archive is "comprised of an inert or immobile collection of documents and files" and demonstrates the effects a variety of actors can have on a mnemonic narrative.[9] Moreover, tangible items like photographs can be identified for the role they play in building a sense of the past.[10] More generally, an affective and successful history can be effected as a product of the materiality of a museum.[11] In relation to Australia, then, one can begin to appreciate that the interplay of ordinary objects, records, and the ordering of artifacts within the Australian War Memorial (AWM) is entangled in a process of enacting mnemonic artifacts that transform into symbols of national importance.

Apprehending memory to be a product of environment also enables one to identify the temporal factors invoked in the enactment of, for instance, a commemorative narrative. A sense of continuity, consistency, and extent of reference to a particular reading of the past are all integral to the performance of a convincing mnemonic story.[12] Of course, we already intuitively know this to be the case; commemorative events are often built around regular and ritualistic performances of the past in order to stage a sense of continuity and, thus, engender a sense of le-

9   Renisa Mawani, "Law's Archive," *Annual Review of Law and Social Science* 8, no. 1 (2012): 348.

10 Elizabeth Edwards, "Photographs and History: Emotion and Materiality," in *Museum Materialities: Objects, Engagements, Interpretations,* ed. Sandra H. Dudley (London: Routledge, 2010), 21–38; Gabriele Schwab, "Replacement Children: The Transgenerational Transmission of Traumatic Loss," in *Memory and Political Change,* eds. Aleida Assmann and Linda Shortt (Basingstoke: Palgrave MacMillan, 2012), 17–33.

11 Sheila Watson, "Myth, Memory and the Senses in the Churchill Museum," in *Museum Materialities: Objects, Engagements, Interpretations,* ed. Sandra H. Dudley (London: Routledge, 2010), 204–23.

12 Jörn Rüsen, *History: Narration, Interpretation, Orientation* (Oxford: Berghahn Books, 2005); Astrid Erll, *Memory in Culture,* trans. Sara B. Young (Basingstoke: Palgrave Macmillan, 2011); Assmann, *Cultural Memory and Early Civilization.*

gitimacy and authority.[13] Indeed, the performance of a history in order to foster a sense of purpose and comprehension of a past can be addressed alongside Jan Assmann's conception of memory.

He presents the idea that memory is the "resuscitation performed by the desire of the group not to allow their dead to disappear but, with the aid of memory, to keep them as members of their community and to take them with them into their *progressive present.*"[14] As such, the temporality of a commemorative pattern is an opportunity to continually reintegrate lives of the past into a narrative that seeks to renew a cohesive sense of tradition and shared memory. In this sense, the temporal aspect of memory is vital; an actor which serves to enact this regularity is not representational but is significant and effective.

Documentaries, non-fiction, and fictional depictions and performances of the past, then, can be thought of as televisual actors which are deployed in the enactment of the past. Indeed, they do give continuing credence to certain canonical historiographies and help secure a particular mnemonic narrative. Of course, an associated responsibility with the recognition of the significant temporal element of memory exists. This responsibility is to question the extent to which the temporal spine of a memory is the medium for the enactment of an exclusionary or incomplete mnemonic story.

Exploring the Truth of Bean's Diaries

As the founder of the AWM, C.E.W. Bean already occupies a prominent place within Australian military history and within

---

13   For more on the link between commemoration and senses of authority, see David Cannadine, "The Context, Performance, and Meaning of Ritual: The British Monarchy and the 'Invention of Tradition,' c. 1820–1977," in *The Invention of Tradition,* eds. Eric Hobsbawm and Terence Ranger (Cambridge: Cambridge University Press, 1983), 101–64.

14   Jan Assmann, *Cultural Memory and Early Civilization: Writing, Remembrance, and Political Imagination* (Cambridge: Cambridge University Press, 2011), 20 (original emphasis).

the Anzac legend. Alongside this, his diarizing of the Anzacs at Gallipoli is an important element of the Anzac commemorative narrative.[15] His motivation for writing these diaries has been identified, most recently in the 2015 documentary series, *The Memorial: Beyond the Anzac Legend,* as the heavy responsibility he felt to tell the story of the Anzacs.[16] The presenter, Neil Oliver, highlights Bean's fastidious approach to historical volumes and the documentation of those who fought. Moreover, the notion that Bean started his diaries as just one man noticing something important taking place and making a note of it so people "did not forget" gives a sense that his work is authentic and organic. Alongside the reliance on historical documentation, his account is thus considered an authoritative source on which the Anzac story can be told. Over 100 years on from Gallipoli, Bean's mediated account of the experiences of the Anzacs retain their strength and veracity today. The prominence of his work in the AWM, and the repetition of the canonical status of his work in documentaries, ensures it.

For instance, the *Beyond the Anzac Legend* documentary series stresses the authority of the sources on which the AWM is built. Alongside Bean's diaries, Oliver considers the written artifacts of war, including letters home or poetry of soldiers. In the perspectival frames introduced in section one, one might say that such documentaries perform the veracity of these sources and help enact them as an integral part of a particular mnemonic narrative. Indeed, an identification of what is engaged in order to effect the strength of these sources of memory and history can usefully be cast on the basis of the post-humanist or ecological ethic considered above.

---

15 For the volumes of the history of Australia in World War I written by Bean, see C.E.W Bean, *Official History of Australia in the War of 1914–1918,* 6 vols. (Sydney: Angus & Robertson, 1921–1942). For selected diary entries, see C.E.W Bean, *Gallipoli Correspondent: The Frontline Diary of C.E.W Bean,* ed. Kevin Fewster (Sydney: Allen & Unwin, 1983).

16 Janine Hosking, ed., *The Memorial: Beyond the Anzac Legend,* feat. Neil Oliver, first aired November 4, 2014, on Foxtel's History Channel.

This ethic encourages us to apprehend what is deployed and should thus be factored into analysis of how memories come to be constituted and sustained. This includes films and both archives and museums, as these can have embedded and constitutive impacts on senses of identity.[17] As such, an explanation of the televisual, cinematic, and archival elements of the Anzac Day narrative is invited. Films, for instance, can be considered a perfect means of adding texture to the bare details of a past event.[18]

This is not least because they affect responses from audiences and communities; they are key to the maintenance of a mythology. Winter recognizes that the power of film is the capacity it has for drawing audiences into particular worlds. It impresses visual messages upon audiences which conform to, and to nourish, a specific narrative. The regularity of the Anzac Day commemoration and the associated deference of fictional films and the life and work of C.E.W. Bean give a sense of ongoing, regularized, and constitutive importance.

Identifying such creative media as "sites" of memory enables one to address these media as loci for the enactment of a narrative.[19] This identification means these sites can be imbued with a sense of instrumentality, or at least contribution, when it comes to effecting a particular narrative. Their identification as sites

---

17 On the impact of film on identity, see, for example, Jaqueline Maingard, "Cinemagoing in District Six, Cape Town, 1920s to 1960s: History, Politics, Memory," *Memory Studies* 10, no. 1 (2017): 17–34. On the role of museums in buttressing senses of community, see Stacy Douglas, "Museums as Constitutions: A Commentary on Constitutions and Constitution Making," *Law, Culture and the Humanities* 11, no. 3 (2015): 349–62.

18 For more on the role of popular media in buttressing memory, see Jay M. Winter, "The Performance of the Past: Memory, History, Identity," in *Performing the Past: Memory, History, and Identity in Modern Europe,* eds. Karin Tilmans, Frank van Vree, and Jay M. Winter (Amsterdam: Amsterdam University Press, 2010), 11–34.

19 Michael Keren, "Commemorating Jewish Martyrdom," in *War Memory and Popular Culture: Essays on Modes of Remembrance and Commemoration,* eds. Michael Keren and Holger H. Herwig (Jefferson: McFarland, 2009), 9–21.

circumvents a difficulty with understanding them on a textual basis. For instance, in relation to memory, Paul Connerton, in *How Modernity Forgets,* considers certain places, sites, as being dynamically conducive to memory, rather than as a medium of representation.

This dynamism, rather than representation, invites an exploration of how each element is deployed in the Anzac story and what is being deployed in order to demonstrate a more complex, more ambiguous, narrative. This narrative is not merely obscured in favor of neatly represented historical and mnemonic "authority" but actively constructed and sustained in such media. For instance, the *Beyond the Anzac Legend* documentary reveres Bean and his diaries for a distinct lack of censorship as being tantamount to authenticity. To some degree, this lack of censorship needs to be applauded, particularly if one compares it with some of Bean's other contemporary curators and archivists.[20] Notwithstanding this supposedly minimal censorship, Bean's diaries do not of course tell the complete picture of Australian involvement in World War I.

Nevertheless, his work is held in high regard as a source of historical accuracy at the AWM and throughout Australia. This sense of accuracy is also depended upon when it comes to the writing of screenplays and the production of films. As far as historical authority goes, Bean's diaries are buttressed and rendered secure, or even canonical, by these sources. For instance, Peter Weir's 1981 film *Gallipoli* can be thought of as a cinematographic extension of the Anzac legend.[21] While one can situate a consideration of this film within a revisionist critique of the accuracy of the history it portrays, it is nevertheless apprehended as believable and both an effective and affective actor within the continuing Anzac narrative.

---

20 Anne-Marie Condé, "John Treloar, Official War Art and the Australian War Memorial," *Australian Journal of Politics & History* 53, no. 3 (2007): 451–64.

21 Peter Weir, dir., *Gallipoli* (Sydney: R&R films, 1981).

This is because "the harsh, dreadful and disturbing realities of war that remain embedded both physically and aesthetically [at Gallipoli]" are engendered by various mediums, including Weir's film.[22] Moreover, such films perform the authority and authenticity of the canonical texts of the Anzac legend because they seek to represent these horrors. This authenticity is also effected in films which do not directly relate the viewer to the experience of Anzac through the protagonist. For example, the film *The Water Diviner* serves to add a textural depth to one brief story from Bean's accounts of a father searching for the remains of his son at Gallipoli.[23] The fact that such films are os-tensibly based on, and corroborate, the tropes present in Bean's diaries that each Anzac was "an ordinary Australian willing to do his duty in extraordinarily difficult circumstances [and, thus] a testament to the rugged stoicism of the average Australian" serves to buttress the status of Bean's diaries as a dependable mnemonic actor.[24]

However, such corroboration serves to brush past an out-standing point to be made about censorship in relation to Bean's diaries and thus the basis of the Anzac commemorative nar-rative. As un(der)censored his diaries may be as far as content goes, his reliance on official records raises some questions. By the time Bean comes to have a use of these records, in order to buttress his diaries and record-keeping, they have already been considerably and meaningfully filtered. A number of people are improperly recorded and, as such, are not properly recognized

22 Nick Osbaldiston and Theresa Petray, "The Role of Horror and Dread in the Sacred Experience," *Tourist Studies* 11, no. 2 (2011): 177.

23 Russel Crowe, dir., *The Water Diviner* (Los Angeles: RatPac Entertain-ment, 2014).

24 Kasun Ubayasiri, "The Anzac Myth and the Shaping of Contemporary Australian War Reportage," *Media, War & Conflict* 8, no. 2 (2015): 217. More generally on this trope in relation to the Anzacs, see Jenny MacLeod, *Reconsidering Gallipoli* (Manchester: Manchester University Press, 2004). Mark McKenna, "Anzac Day: How Did It Become Australia's National Day?" in *What's Wrong with ANZAC?: The Militarisation of Australian His-tory,* eds. Marylin Lake and Henry Reynolds (Sydney: University of New South Wales Press, 2010), 110–34.

in official records. This lack of recognition is hardly pressed, in favor of extolling the virtues of Bean's lack of censorship. It raises important questions about the values of historical truth and the authenticity of a mnemonic narrative.

Despite their marginalization, Aboriginal and Torres Strait Islanders contributed to the Australian war effort, volunteering to join the Anzacs. However, at the time, racially motivated legislation in Australia did prevent Aboriginal and Torres Strait Islanders from volunteering.[25] To circumvent this law, they had to falsely represent themselves as being of significantly European descent. Reference was made to this during the *Beyond the Anzac Legend* documentary, during a tangential exploration of the bravery of an Aboriginal volunteer conducted by members of the AWM.

A lot was made of this discovery, as it was a rare instance of an Aboriginal Australian being decorated during World War I. However, as his family suggest within this feature, he "looked European" and would have used his appearance to deceive his way into volunteering for the Anzacs. This point was not pressed, but it raises significant questions about both the purposeful and ancillary rejection of Aboriginal involvement which still pervades within the Anzac legend. Of course, a greater degree of recognition of Aboriginal involvement during World War I and, thus, constitutive of the Anzac legend, is now beginning to exist in the Anzac narrative. There are still questions to be asked about how they are recognized in the "more inclusive" narrative. Notwithstanding the increased recognition and the associated problematization of it, it is important to note that Bean's collected diaries are still a prominent element of the Anzac legend.

This prominence is engineered through displays in museums, consideration in documentaries, and use as an informative and authoritative source in film and televisual accounts of the Anzacs. As such, what is ultimately an exclusionary authority on

---

25 Philippa Scarlett, "Aboriginal Service in the First World War: Identity, Recognition, and the Problem of Mateship," *Aboriginal History Journal* 39 (2015): 163–81.

the Anzac legend is being performed. Insistence on the reverence shown towards such sources sustains a Eurocentric, or Euro-exclusive, narrative. Such a direct and underexplored feature of the Anzac narrative is unfortunate. Moreover, it is positively harmful when relatable to exclusions of Aboriginal servicepeople from Anzac Day marches and from global recognition during the commemoration of a significant milestone.[26]

A greater commitment, or responsibility, toward examining the details of elements of a commemorative story, as opposed to uncritical reverence, offers an opportunity to challenge and rethink a secured narrative. For instance, if Bean's diaries were assessed for their historical specificity and contingency rather than their sense of authenticity and purity, a more inclusive narrative may be made more possible. As it is, the truth of Bean's diaries is embedded in the work done by a number of other supporting actors. The performativity of such truth in his diaries also begets the performativity of the truth and inviolability of a commemorative narrative. As such, attunement toward exploring the process by which something comes to be rendered true, authoritative, and convincing reflects a commitment to blurring the distinction between truth and untruth.

Given that memories, like history, are thought to mediate collective imaginaries and give authority to our actions in particular situations, there are clear social and political consequences for problematizing mnemonic and historical "truth."[27] An aspect of more responsible positioning towards the study of

---

26 Biwa Kwan, "Indigenous Australians Mark Anzac Day," sbs News, April 26, 2015, http://www.sbs.com.au/news/article/2015/04/26/indigenous-australians-mark-anzac-day. The bbc covered, and offered a commentary on, a special commemorative event at the Cenotaph in Whitehall, marking the 100th anniversary of the Gallipoli landings and the origin of the Anzac story. Despite recognition of the Gurkhas and Māori, no room in the commemorative program was set aside for the commemoration or recognition of Aboriginal and Torres Strait Islander contributions to the Anzac legend.

27 Nutsa Batiashvili, "The 'Myth' of the Self: The Georgian National Narrative and Quest for 'Georgianness,'" in Memory and Political Change, eds. Aleida Assmann and Linda Shortt (Basingstoke: Palgrave Macmillan, 2012), 186–200.

memory, then, is a commitment to articulating its dynamism and pluralism precisely because memory, agency, and social obligations are bound together.[28] The dynamism suggested of memory means that it can be thought of as a produced effect. In doing so, it is opened up to methodologies which seek to examine how something is constituted or "in the works."

In other words, it is important to reveal how precarious certain truths are, because they are always a product of work that goes into securing them. Such a performance of truth may have hitherto gone uncovered.[29] The more one seeks to explore the precarity and vulnerability of an element of a particular system — its reliance on a number of other things for its strength — one can begin to acknowledge its "taken-for-granted-ness" rather than unadulterated accuracy.

Broadly, then, responsibility to the study of memory can be expressed as a commitment to complexity, not least because there is so much at stake as far as mnemonic narratives go. While this section and chapter has focused solely and briefly on Bean's diaries, it has served to demonstrate the broader point about the situatedness of both a mnemonic narrative and the features that come to constitute it. One might argue that this is particularly pertinent in relation to a textual element of a mnemonic narrative because memory is significantly mediated by literacy.[30] Indeed, Jens Brockmeier suggests there is no place or evident boundedness to memory.[31] Rather, bringing the moral of Brockmeier's work back into a post-humanist vocabulary, it is an agency distributed across a number of things. As such, mining each of these things for information about their own

---

28 On the entanglement of memory and both senses of agency and social obligation, see, for example, Erll, *Memory in Culture.*

29 See, especially for his analogous exploration of how scientific rules come to be settled upon rather than merely exhibited, Bruno Latour, *The Pasteurization of France,* trans. Alan Sheridan and John Law (Cambridge: Harvard University Press, 1988).

30 Jens Brockmeier, *Beyond the Archive: Memory, Narrative, and the Autobiographical Process* (Oxford: Oxford University Press, 2015).

31 Ibid.

constitution necessarily impacts upon what we know and think of a mnemonic narrative.

Conclusion: Responsibility and Memory

This chapter has briefly touched upon one small element of the Anzac commemorative story, in order to articulate how memories should actually be thought of as a product of a lot of work, rather than as a representation of a shared truth. For instance, in relation to Bean's diaries, one can identify how film and documentary are embroiled in the enactment of a compelling narrative. One can argue that the narrative is compelling, to borrow from Bruno Latour, because it holds together and is *being* held together.[32] The consequence for thinking about memory in this way is an appreciation that a memory's normative and formative power is an enactment, rather than stable and indisputable. As such, one must explore the possibilities in addressing how a mnemonic narrative might be shifted and what the implications of this shift might be for social and political organization. Given that the ties between social and political organization and memory, in various guises, has been made, the purposive responsibility to problematize memory and the memories around which communities are oriented can be made.[33]

But beyond the direct link between community constitution and memory, one can also approach the obligation to remember on the basis of the virtue of remembering. Jeffrey Blustein makes this point when he suggests that we can think of memory

---

32 Latour, *The Pasteurization of France.*

33 For an example of critical reflection on the power of forms of memory in the construction of forms of political community see Eric Hobsbawm, "Mass-Producing Traditions: Europe, 1870–1914," in *The Invention of Tradition,* eds. Eric Hobsbawm and Terence Ranger (Cambridge: Cambridge University Press, 1983), 263–308. Aleida Assmann and Linda Shortt, "Memory and Political Change: Introduction," in *Memory and Political Change,* eds. Aleida Assmann and Linda Shortt (Basingstoke: Palgrave Macmillan, 2012), 1–14.

beyond consequentialist ethical grounds.[34] A non-consequentialist impression of remembrance suggests, for Blustein, that it is a valuable commitment in and of itself. So, notwithstanding what a more inclusive mnemonic narrative might mean for the greater recognition of Aboriginal and Torres Strait Islanders in Australia, there is deep value in more detailed, complex, and perhaps more challenging remembrance of an event or history for its own sake.

So, the duty related to collective remembrance may not necessarily need to be cast on the basis of what social and moral obligations might be effected by a shift in a mnemonic narrative but the social and moral obligation to remember more fully. So, "lest we forget" can be thought of less as a duty not to forget for the purposes of a particular purpose of moral goal but not to forget at all. At this stage, I think one can suggest that a greater commitment to not forgetting should also be opened up to the things which may have previously gone forgotten.

---

34 Jeffrey Blustein, "How the Past Matters: On the Foundations of an Ethics of Remembrance," in *Historical Justice and Memory*, eds. Klaus Neumann and Janna Thompson (Madison: University of Wisconsin Press, 2015), 74–92.

Bibliography

Assmann, Aleida, and Linda Shortt. "Memory and Political Change: Introduction." In *Memory and Political Change,* edited by Aleida Assmann and Linda Shortt, 1–14. Basingstoke: Palgrave Macmillan, 2012.

Assmann, Jan. *Cultural Memory and Early Civilization: Writing, Remembrance, and Political Imagination.* Cambridge: Cambridge University Press, 2011.

Batiashvili, Nutsa. "The 'Myth' of the Self: The Georgian National Narrative and Quest for 'Georgianness.'" In *Memory and Political Change,* edited by Aleida Assmann and Linda Shortt, 186–200. Basingstoke: Palgrave Macmillan, 2012.

Bean, C.E.W. *Gallipoli Correspondent: The Frontline Diary of C.E.W Bean,* edited by Kevin Fewster. Sydney: Allen & Unwin, 1983.

———. *Official History of Australia in the War of 1914–1918.* 6 vols. Sydney: Angus & Robertson, 1921–1942.

Blustein, Jeffrey. "How the Past Matters: On the Foundations of an Ethics of Remembrance." In *Historical Justice and Memory,* edited by Klaus Neumann and Janna Thompson, 74–92. Madison: University of Wisconsin Press, 2015.

Brockmeier, Jens. *Beyond the Archive: Memory, Narrative, and the Autobiographical Process.* Oxford: Oxford University Press, 2015.

Cannadine, David. "The Context, Performance, and Meaning of Ritual: The British Monarchy and the 'Invention of Tradition', c. 1820–1977." In *The Invention of Tradition,* edited by Eric Hobsbawm and Terence Ranger, 101–64. Cambridge: Cambridge University Press, 1983.

Condé, Anne-Marie. "John Treloar, Official War Art and the Australian War Memorial." *Australian Journal of Politics & History* 53, no. 3 (2007): 451–64. DOI: 10.1111/j.1467-8497.2007.00469.x.

Connerton, Paul. *How Modernity Forgets.* Cambridge: Cambridge University Press, 2009.

Crowe, Russell, dir. *The Water Diviner.* Los Angeles: RatPac Entertainment, 2014.

Dorsett, Shaunnagh, and Shaun McVeigh. *Jurisdiction.* London: Routledge, 2012.

Douglas, Stacy. "Museums as Constitutions: A Commentary on Constitutions and Constitution Making." Law, *Culture and the Humanities* 11, no. 3 (2015): 349–62. DOI: 10.1177/1743872113499226.

Edwards, Elizabeth. "Photographs and History: Emotion and Materiality." In *Museum Materialities: Objects, Engagements, Interpretations,* edited by Sandra H. Dudley, 21–38. London: Routledge, 2010.

Erll, Astrid. *Memory in Culture.* Translated by Sara B. Young. Basingstoke: Palgrave Macmillan, 2011.

Halbwachs, Maurice. *On Collective Memory.* Edited and translated by Lewis A. Coser. Chicago: University of Chicago Press, 1992.

Hobsbawm, Eric. "Mass-Producing Traditions: Europe, 1870–1914." In *The Invention of Tradition,* edited by Eric Hobsbawm and Terence Ranger, 263–308. Cambridge: Cambridge University Press, 1983.

Hosking, Janine, dir. *Memorial: Beyond the Anzac Legend.* First aired November 4, 2014, on Foxtel's History Channel (Australia).

Hoskins, Andrew. "Memory Ecologies." *Memory Studies* 9, no. 3 (2016): 348–57. DOI: 10.1177/1750698016645274.

Keren, Michael. "Commemorating Jewish Martyrdom." In *War Memory and Popular Culture: Essays on Modes of Remembrance and Commemoration,* edited by Michael Keren and Holger H. Herwig, 9–21. Jefferson: McFarland, 2009.

Kwan, Biwa. "Indigenous Australians Mark Anzac Day." *SBS News,* April 26, 2015. http://www.sbs.com.au/news/article/2015/04/26/indigenous-australians-mark-anzac-day.

Latour, Bruno. *Reassembling the Social: An Introduction to Actor-Network-Theory.* Oxford: Oxford University Press, 2005.

———. *The Pasteurization of France.* Translated by Alan Sheridan and John Law. Cambridge: Harvard University Press, 1988.

MacLeod, Jenny. *Reconsidering Gallipoli.* Manchester: Manchester University Press, 2004.

Maingard, Jaqueline. "Cinemagoing in District Six, Cape Town, 1920s to 1960s: History, Politics, Memory." *Memory Studies* 10, no. 1 (2017): 17–34. DOI: 10.1177/1750698016670786.

Mawani, Renisa. "Law's Archive." *Annual Review of Law and Social Science* 8, no. 1 (2012): 337–65. DOI: 10.1146/annurev-lawsocsci-102811-173900.

McKenna, Mark. "Anzac Day: How Did It Become Australia's National Day?" In *What's Wrong with ANZAC? The Militarisation of Australian History,* edited by Marylin Lake and Henry Reynolds, 110–34. Sydney: University of New South Wales Press, 2010.

Olick, Jeffrey K. "Collective Memory: The Two Cultures." *Sociological Theory* 17, no. 3 (1999): 333–48. DOI: 10.1111/0735-2751.00083.

Osbaldiston, Nick, and Theresa Petray. "The Role of Horror and Dread in the Sacred Experience." *Tourist Studies* 11, no. 2 (2011): 175–90. DOI: 10.1177/1468797611424955.

Radley, Alan. "Artefacts, Memory, and a Sense of the Past." In *Collective Remembering,* edited by David Middleton and Derek Edwards, 46–59. London: Sage Publications, 1990.

Rüsen, Jörn. *History: Narration, Interpretation, Orientation.* Oxford: Berghahn Books, 2005.

Scarlett, Philippa. "Aboriginal Service in the First World War: Identity, Recognition, and the Problem of Mateship." *Aboriginal History Journal* 39 (2015): 163–81. DOI: 10.22459/AH.39.2015.08.

Schwab, Gabriele. "Replacement Children: The Transgenerational Transmission of Traumatic Loss." In *Memory and Political Change,* edited by Aleida Assmann and Linda Shortt, 17–33. Basingstoke: Palgrave MacMillan, 2012.

Shotter, John. "The Social Construction of Remembering and
    Forgetting." In *Collective Remembering*, edited by David
    Middleton and Derek Edwards, 120–38. London: Sage
    Publications, 1990.

Ubayasiri, Kasun. "The Anzac Myth and the Shaping
    of Contemporary Australian War Reportage."
    Media, War & Conflict 8, no. 2 (2015): 213–28. DOI:
    10.1177/1750635215584282.

Watson, Sheila. "Myth, Memory and the Senses in the
    Churchill Museum." In *Museum Materialities: Objects,
    Engagements, Interpretations,* edited by Sandra H. Dudley,
    204–23. London: Routledge, 2010.

Weir, Peter, dir. *Gallipoli.* Sydney: R&R films, 1981.

Winter, Jay M. "The Performance of the Past: Memory,
    History, Identity." In *Performing the Past: Memory, History,
    and Identity in Modern Europe,* edited by Karin Tilmans,
    Frank van Vree, and Jay M. Winter, 11–34. Amsterdam:
    Amsterdam University Press, 2010.

5

Bodies

Rosalie Metro

People are trapped in history, and history is trapped in them.
— James Baldwin

Envision a clear fall morning in a small city in the midwestern United States.[1] A parade winds through town. Blond children wave at the marching band. A red convertible crawls along the road, carrying a man of importance. Suddenly, a group of Black students emerges from the crowd and links arms in the road, blocking the convertible's path. One of them raises a bullhorn to his lips.

What happens next? How do people know what to do, what to say? The protest was planned, but the crowd's reaction could not be. People are called upon to react spontaneously, but I will argue they are also called upon to remember. Because it is not 1965, it is 2015.

1   I would like to thank Feliticas Macgilchrist and Roman Richtera for their helpful comments on an earlier draft of this chapter. I also want to express my deep gratitude to Reuben Faloughi, a participant in the protest I describe, for his feedback on this chapter. To Reuben and all those connected with cs1950, thank you for putting your hearts, minds, and bodies at risk to help our community confront the ongoing brutality of racism.

If, as James Baldwin says, history is trapped in people,[2] it is trapped not only in their minds, but also in their bodies. This corporeal memory, even more than cerebral memory, connects individuals with identity groups and shared histories. When academics talk about memory, they usually focus on what people think.[3] But what do people do? When the past is suddenly thrust into view, how do people honor or suppress it using the blunt instruments they have at hand — their bodies, their voices, their gestures?

The white man in the red convertible was Tim Wolfe, President of the University of Missouri. The students called themselves "Concerned Student 1950" (or CS1950), a reference to the first year the university admitted a Black student. The Homecoming Parade, usually a celebration of school spirit and athletic prowess, became an impromptu history classroom, as CS1950 recited a timeline of racist events beginning with the university's founding as a school for white men in 1839. Wolfe sat silently throughout this demonstration. Many of the (mostly white) bystanders attempted to drown out the students' voices with chants of their own, and several of them intervened physically by linking arms and standing between the protesters and Tim Wolfe's car. After twelve minutes, the police forcibly dispersed the students and the parade moved forward.

This demonstration was not the beginning of racial tension at the university's flagship campus in Columbia nor was it the end. Rather, it could be seen as a continuation of the timeline the students recited. Over the next few weeks, in a series of events that garnered national media spotlight, the protests gained momentum. On November 9th, less than a month after the Homecoming Parade, Tim Wolfe resigned.

In the flurry of media coverage that followed Wolfe's resignation, commentators looked back at the Homecoming Parade protest in order to understand these historic and controversial

---

2   James Baldwin, "Stranger in the Village," *Harper's Magazine*, October 1953.

3   Rafael F. Narvaez, "Embodiment, Collective Memory and Time," *Body & Society* 12, no. 3 (2006): 5–73.

events. Commentary centers on a video shot by a protester, which has been viewed on YouTube almost half a million times.[4] This video is polysemic: viewers make meaning of it in radically different ways, using it as evidence to support a range of conclusions. We all watch the same video but not through the same eyes.

In this chapter, I will analyze the social semiotics of the Homecoming Parade demonstration through a multimodal analysis of the video. I conceptualize cs1950's recitation of a timeline as a "memory practice" in which the protesters force Wolfe and the spectators to bear witness to a history of racism that has been "whitewashed" from traditional academic spaces. The protesters act out of memory lodged in their bodies, making meaning with the raw material of sound and flesh. Wolfe and the mostly white onlookers cannot help but respond in kind, letting collective memory animate their bodies and voices.

In watching the video, and in reading (or, in my case, writing) this chapter, we are drawn irresistibly into a process of semiosis that implicates us in the power dynamics of race. We are spectators, but in making sense of the demonstration, we become participants. There is no neutral point from which to observe, nowhere to stand that does not involve "taking a stand."

Memory Studies and Corporeality

Scholars of contemporary memory studies often focus on the technologies that people use to preserve the past. Geoffrey C. Bowker, for instance, catalogues the social practices and physical objects we use to construct "memory regimes" from the chaotic past.[5] He points out that the technologies we use, from the archive of file folders to the massive digital spaces that have opened in the past few decades, shape the knowledge that we re-

---

4   Concerned Student, "1839 Built on Our Black Homecoming Parade Demonstration," *YouTube,* October 13, 2015, https://www.youtube.com/watch?v=u6zwnmlzZSQ.

5   Geoffrey C. Bowker, *Memory Practices in the Sciences* (Cambridge: MIT Press, 2005), 10.

cord. But he does not focus on the oldest way of holding knowledge — in the body.

Rafael Narvaez draws attention to this oversight in memory
studies by bringing together the work of French sociologists
Maurice Halbwachs, Emile Durkheim, and Marcel Mauss in
order to discover how embodied collective memory functions.
Challenging Cartesian mind–body duality, Narvaez defines
bodies as "mnemonic media for the social."[6] Most relevant to
my inquiry is his approach to race, which he defines "not as an
aspect of nature but a process whereby inherited collective ideas
become internalized, naturalized, and sedimented within the
domain of embodied collective memory."[7] Using the example of
race, he argues that embodied collective memories can "channel
the past," "deflect the past," and even "render history discontinu-
ous," opening the way for new social structures.[8]

Social Semiotics and Multimodal Analysis

If the body is a medium for collective memory, how do we interpret what bodies do? Social semiotics is the study of signs,
what they mean, and how people use them to communicate.[9]
Multimodal analysis is a method of interpreting data that can
reveal social semiotics. While discourse analysis often overlooks
what is unspoken, multimodal analysis allows researchers to interpret a richer set of data. Multimodal researchers analyze how
people use a range of "semiotic resources," including gesture,
gaze, dress, posture, tone of voice, and even silence. People "or-
chestrate their meaning" by choosing and combining verbal and
non-verbal modes that contribute to meaning.[10]

---

6   Narvaez, "Embodiment, Collective Memory and Time," 62.
7   Rafael F. Narvaez, *Embodied Collective Memory: The Making and Unmak-
    ing of Human Nature* (Lanham: University Press of America, 2013), 109.
8   Ibid.
9   Phillip Vannini, "Social Semiotics and Fieldwork: Methods and Analytics,"
    Qualitative Inquiry 13, no. 1 (2007): 113–40.
10 Carey Jewitt, "An Introduction to Multimodality," in *The Routledge Hand-
    book of Multimodal Analysis,* ed. Carey Jewitt (New York: Routledge, 2014),

Multimodal analysis is particularly appropriate for study-ing memory practices and the politics of identity, which are complex, performative, and socially situated. In education, my primary field of study, researchers use multimodal analysis to probe the meaning of interactions in the classroom.[11] I present a multimodal analysis of this video in the spirit of "disrupting" traditional qualitative inquiry in education by rethinking what counts as data, and what counts as an "educational setting."[12] In this way, I hope to blur the boundaries between scholarship on education and investigations of memory practices.

How does multimodal analysis work? To use an example from the video, protesters wear black t-shirts emblazoned with the outline of a fist, and at several points, they each raise one fist in the air. The raised fist, then, is a sign in modes of gesture and dress. The sign has three parts. The sign vehicle is sometimes the flesh and bones of the hand and sometimes the fabric and color of the t-shirt. The object or concept that is signified could be the Black Power movement and Afrocentrism. The interpretant, or the sense that an observer makes of the relation between the sign vehicle of the raised fist and its object, could be an inspira-tion to struggle for civil rights, for someone sympathetic to the protest; or it could be a disturbing threat to "law and order" for someone unsympathetic to the protest.

All signs are open to multiple interpretations, but they do not mean everything, anything, or nothing.[13] The sign's "actual semiotic potential" is restricted to "the uses that are known by specific users with specific needs in specific contexts."[14] In other

---

16.

11 For example, see Rachel Pinnow, "An Ecology of Fear: Examining the Contradictory Surveillance Terrain Navigated by Mexican Youth in a U.S. Middle School," *Anthropology & Education Quarterly* 44, no. 3 (2013): 253–68.

12 Ruth Nicole Brown, Rozana Carducci, and Candace R. Kuby, *Disrupt-ing Qualitative Inquiry: Possibilities and Tensions in Educational Research* (New York: Peter Lang, 2014).

13 Jewitt, "An Introduction to Multimodality," 29.

14 Vannini, "Social Semiotics and Fieldwork," 119.

words, the analysis of the raised fist that I presented is both mine and not-only-mine.

Furthermore, meaning is context-dependent. A raised fist means something different in Columbia, Missouri, in 2015, in the 1968 Mexico City Olympics, and in ancient Assyria — even if these meanings are related. Finally, meaning is "multiplicative rather than additive," in that modes interact to become more than a sum of their parts.[15] For instance, the gesture of the raised fist, multiplied by the brown skin of the man taking the action, multiplied by his shouts of "POWER!" yielded the analysis above; a white child raising her fist in a classroom might just be trying to get her teacher's attention.

The meanings we make of signs are not "correct" or "incorrect," but meaning can be confirmed or disconfirmed by other observers or by the sign-maker. However, not all interpretations are equally valued. Semiosis is conducted by specific people whose social position matters. In that sense, it is inherently political; meaning comes from power, rather than vice versa.[16] My analysis will demonstrate that the interpretation of signs is politically polarized, so that one sign is taken to have opposite meanings by groups of observers who compete for discursive authority.

This observation brings me to my own positionality. I have lived in Columbia, Missouri since 2009, and I am currently an assistant teaching professor at the university. I attended the Homecoming Parade, though I did not see the demonstration transpire. Whether my position as an observer legitimizes or delegitimizes my process of semiosis will depend on readers' own positions. The validity of my analysis depends not on whether it is correct but on whether it is *convincing* and *whom* it convinces.

---

15 Rosie Flewitt et al., "What Are Multimodal Data and Transcription?," in *The Routledge Handbook of Multimodal Analysis,* ed. Carey Jewitt (New York: Routledge, 2014), 52.

16 Vannini, "Social Semiotics and Fieldwork," 115.

Also, I am white, and my analysis is situated in a social hierarchy that I see as pervasively racist against Black people. As may already be clear, I am sympathetic to the demonstrators and I support their actions as an appropriate form of protest. I was among the crowd supporting CS1950 on the day Wolfe resigned. I mention these details because studying social semiotics requires me to attend to the ways in which "power dynamics — from the moment of research design to that of publication and reception — are not extraneous to research practices."[17] My perspective is limited by so many factors, including my racial identity, that it was important for me to conduct what anthropologists call a "member check."[18] That is why I invited a member of the CS1950 group who was involved in the events I described to read a draft of this chapter and share feedback on it (although I am responsible for any weaknesses in my interpretation). I was not able to conduct a member check with any of the white people who stepped in to counter the protest, so my analysis of their actions is unsubstantiated by them — and I am almost sure they would disagree with it. Yet in writing this chapter, I am not so much making an argument as I am inviting you to confirm or disconfirm my analysis and to enrich my understanding with your own semiotic practices.

How did I analyze the video? In order to observe how modes of gesture and speech worked together, I isolated them and observed their interaction. After viewing the video with sound several times, I listened to the audio track alone. I also watched the video with the sound off to focus on gesture. In this manner, I built up a transcript in layers, separating out the voices from the images and ambient sounds.

The process of analyzing multimodal data should be understood not merely as transcription, but rather as "transduction" from modes including gesture, dress, spoken language, and pos-

---

17 Ibid., 121.
18 Egon G. Guba and Yvonne S. Lincoln. "Competing Paradigms in Qualitative Research." In *The Landscape of Qualitative Research*, eds. Norman K. Denzin and Yvonna S. Lincoln. (Thousand Oaks: Sage, 1994).

ture into written language, images, diagrams, or whatever form researchers use to present conclusions to their audience.[19] Following Gunther Kress, I use graphic means (**bolding** to show emphasis and emotional intensity, SIZE to indicate volume, s p a c i n g to show speed) to approximate sound when transducing speech into words on the page.[20] For instance, at :57 on the video, a female protester says something I transcribe as "this instiTUtion was for W H I T E M E N ONLY, **ON~LY** WHITE MEN." I capitalize stressed syllables, and I use the marker ~ to indicate where her voice cracked with emotion and the strain of shouting. I use the body as a point of reference to convey how gesture is realized in both temporal and spatial dimensions: at 2:08, I note, "tall male protester raises his fist briefly straight into the air above his head, shouting, 'POWER!'"[21] I also approximate the phonemics of African American Vernacular English (AAVE), which some of the protesters use; it is important to note that AAVE is not an "incorrect" version of Standard English, but a non-standard dialect with systematic differences in phonology, morphology, and syntax.[22] But as I am not fluent in this dialect, I may have made errors in transcribing it.

It should be clear that transduction is not a "scientific" methods. Other observers would notice details that I have passed over or would transduce the data differently. It is also important to remember that the video is not an unbiased record of "what happened." The videographer aims her gaze at what compels her, and we are restricted to what we can see through her lens.

Furthermore, the medium of video does not grant us access to all modes, for instance, odor. Because I was present on the day of the parade, I remember the smell of candy that hung in the air that day. All along the parade route, participants tossed

19 Flewitt et. al., "What Are Multimodal Data and Transcription?" 52.

20 Gunther Kress, "What Is Mode?" in *The Routledge Handbook of Multimodal Analysis,* ed. Carey Jewitt (New York: Routledge, 2014), 61.

21 Ibid., 62.

22 "African American Vernacular English," *Portland State University,* 2020, https://www.pdx.edu/multicultural-topics-communication-sciences-disorders/african-american-vernacular-english-aave

sweets to the spectators, and in the sun, they exuded a scent I identified with innocence. The smell signaled the presence of children, who can be seen in the video, and it contributed to the benign mood that the protesters sought to disrupt. Recalling the smells of the parade reminds me how much video — or any medium — leaves out. With those caveats in mind, I will analyze three moments below.

Show Your Colors

In the mode of dress, one trend that is apparent in the first few seconds of the video is that a large percentage of the spectators wear clothing and accessories that are black and "gold" (yellow), the school colors of the University of Missouri. Some of this gear is adorned with the words "Missouri," its nickname "Mizzou," or the Tiger, the university's mascot. Such gear is popular among Columbia residents and university students alike, especially on game days or at events such as the Homecoming Parade, which emphasize school spirit. While athletics in general are popular, Missouri's football program is especially successful. In one sense, then, black and gold clothing unifies the multiracial, although predominantly white, crowd. In the context of sports and school spirit, a common conceit is that skin color does not matter — all Mizzou students and fans are "Tigers" regardless of their race.

This illusion of unity breaks down throughout the course of the video. In the first few minutes of the demonstration, spectators begin shouting "M-I-Z/Z-O-U," a call-and-response chant commonly heard at sporting events. This chant is usually turned against opposing sports teams: one half of the stadium will call out the first three letters, and the other half of the stadium will respond with the last three. In deploying this chant to drown out the protesters' voices, the crowd spontaneously forms a "united front" that "others" the Black demonstrators, marginalizes their concerns, and foregrounds the supposed harmony of a "colorblind" community. This vocal devotion to Mizzou by a crowd of gold-and-black-garbed spectators conveys the message that the demonstrators are traitors to their own institution.[23]

Yet race does matter. In 2015, Black people made up more than half of the football team, yet they represented only seven percent of the student body as a whole and eleven percent of the state's population.[24] This discrepancy reflects an academic opportunity gap among racial groups, and it also perpetuates the trope of the Black entertainer/athlete. Players usually receive full scholarships in exchange for their athletic labor, but the value of these scholarships is a tiny fraction of what the team earns for the university. The coach is the school's highest-paid employee with a salary of four million dollars a year. Given these conditions, white spectators' attempts to drown out the protesters' voices with chants of "M-I-Z/Z-O-U" can be interpreted as an attempt to put Black students "in their place" as athletes who should bolster school spirit and work for the common good rather than naysayers who challenge the university's claims to inclusivity.

Mizzou's Black football players simultaneously confirmed this interpretation of the social semiotics of the demonstration and resisted the white spectators' deployment of sports-related signifiers of unity several weeks later. Players tweeted a photo of themselves in black-and-gold gear, arms linked. They expressed their support of a protester who had, by that point, gone on hunger strike to underscore CS1950's demands. They announced that they would not play football until Tim Wolfe resigned, placing the university at risk of paying a million-dollar fine to their next scheduled opponents.[25] The football players' action, which

---

23 The Tigers take their name from a militia that defended Columbia against Confederate-allied groups during the Civil War; rivals, the Kansas City Jayhawks, take their name from pro-slavery forces. These mascots subtly connote the violent history of race relations in the US, which white fans refer to in jest as a "border war," while bracketing out the relevance of racism to contemporary life.

24 "Student Enrollment Data," *University of Missouri*, 2019, https://enroll-ment.missouri.edu/reports-data/

25 "Black Mizzou Players Say They'll Strike until President Tim Wolfe Resigns," ESPN, November 7, 2015, http://www.espn.com/college-football/

was supported by their white coach and white teammates, ret-rospectively bolstered the demonstrators' voices. In this way, the protesters and their supporters attempted to reclaim the semiotic value of the colors black and gold: instead of signifying the "colorblind" unity demanded by whites, they repurposed Mizzou gear to represent the solidarity of Black students and the economic power Black athletes held.

Move On!

Several minutes into the demonstration, spectators start calling out, "Move On!" This refrain could be interpreted as a command to the protesters to physically move off of the parade route, or it could be an exhortation to psychically move beyond the instances of racism that they are recounting. This excerpt illustrates both usages:

> 2:47 White blond woman in crowd waves her hand away from her body repeatedly, then turns her face away from cs1950 protester Autumn: "**Move on!**" Others in crowd: "Move on!" White woman in grey shirt crouches down by a young boy.

> 2:49 Autumn: "**I'm sorry**, we are NOT going to **move on**, I'm sorry, you just gonna have to **deal wit it**…oKAY?" She gestures with her hand toward her own body emphatically several times.

> 2:53 videographer's thumb over lens

> 2:59 Autumn: "he **SUED-shhh**—" (raises her hand, brings it down — in frustration?) "He ~SUED the University of Missouri, and soon after, he **WON his ~CASE**"

story/_/id/14078494/missouri-tigers-football-players-strike-embattled-tim-wolfe-resigns.

117

3:04 videographer: "You got it, baby. **YOU GOT IT, AUTUMN!**"

3:10 Autumn: "ASHE!"[26] cs1950: "POWER!" Autumn: "ASHE!" cs1950: "POWER!" Autumn: "ASHE!" cs1950: "POWER!" (videographer joins in on POWER). Tall protester raises his fist briefly. Autumn hands the bullhorn to protester Drea.

3:12 White man in baseball cap and black sweatshirt points away and shouts: "**Move on!**"

3:16 Drea, quietly, quickly: "1939, Lucile Bluford petitioned to get into the graduate school at the University of Missouri — "

3:19 woman in crowd: "It's 2015, **move on!**"

3:20 Drea, calmly, to someone in crowd behind videographer: "It's okay, we just trying to **educate** you, thass all, thass no harm at all."

3:24 videographer: "Don't even enGAGE, don't even **enGAGE with IGnorance!**"

3:31 Drea: "after that she was admitted to the university but she was not allowed to enroll in any classes at the university."

In the first instance, when the blond woman uses the phrase "Move on!" accompanied by a repeated wave, she seems to want to the protesters to physically move away from her. After she speaks, she turns her face away; if the protesters will not move, she will deny them her attention. Autumn confronts this woman by insisting that cs1950 will not "move on," but the woman's words seem to disturb her. Her voice breaks with emotion, and she pauses in order to collect herself, or perhaps to prevent her-

---

26 *Ashe* is a Yoruba word meaning "power."

self from deviating further from the script of the historical time-line. Although Autumn and the blond woman never touch each other, their confrontation is reflected in their body language and the emotional intensity of their voices.

In contrast, several seconds later, Drea argues with another spectator on a more intellectual level. The unseen woman who calls out, "it's 2015, move on!" seems to echo the sentiments of the person who shouts, "get a life!" at 1:12. She is mocking the protesters for dwelling on historical instances of racism that she sees as having no contemporary relevance. Drea responds to the heckler's words by clarifying her intention to educate the specta-tors and asserting that the education she offers is harmless. Her tone is calm, almost conciliatory.

One element that connects these two uses of the phrase "move on" is the dialectic between what the protesters call "edu-cation" and "ignorance." Ignorance is not just being unaware of the timeline of racism that cs1950 seeks to present, it is an ac-tive attempt to ignore, to physically turn away from these events. This section of the video illustrates that cs1950 is engaging in a memory practice intended to "educate" "ignorant," white spec-tators. cs1950 was certainly aware that many spectators would resist this educative process; hence, they engage in civil disobe-dience that forces their audience to listen and share a space with them, instead of, for example, creating a Black History float as a sanctioned part of the parade.

Link Arms

At :34, cs1950 protesters link arms, and they remain in this po-sition for the majority of the demonstration. In doing so, they tap into a vocabulary of protest that dates to the Civil Rights era, when Black leaders including Dr. Martin Luther King, Jr. used this technique as a way of passively resisting police and counterdemonstrators. One iconic photo from the 1963 "March on Washington" shows Black and white demonstrators link-ing hands across their bodies. Linking arms both signifies the solidarity of the protesters and creates a practical obstacle to authorities who wish to disperse a demonstration — it can be read as a gesture of protection against intruders or opponents. It also marks who is part of a demonstration versus who is a bystander. In the past few years, activists from the Black Lives Matter movement have taken up this gesture as part of their effort to resist police misconduct against Black people.[27]

Yet the gesture of linked arms does not symbolize non-violence to all observers. In 2011, when Occupy Wall Street protesters at the University of California-Berkeley linked arms as part of their protest of the school's complicity in economic inequality, the Chancellor argued that the gesture signified violence.[28] In its criticism of the university, the American Civil Liberties Union noted the legacy of linked arms in peaceful protests.[29] This dissonance shows that the gesture's meaning is contested: to those in power, it can be perceived as a threat to both physical and institutional structures, whereas to protesters and their sympathizers, it is evidence of a demonstration's peaceful nature.

At 7:10, white spectators appropriate the gesture of linked arms, inserting themselves between CS1950 protesters and Tim Wolfe's car. Several men, led by a man in a white shirt who has been among the most vocal opponents of the protest, link arms with two women who emerge from the crowd — the older woman with blond hair who had called out "move on!" at 2:47 and a younger woman who had at that juncture been crouching down to speak to a boy.

What do the white spectators seek to protect by linking arms? The man in the white shirt clarifies what is at stake by saying,

---

27 Ferguson, Missouri, the site of 2014 unrest following the killing of unarmed, Black teen Michael Brown by a white officer, is just a two-hour drive from Columbia. Some CS1950 members had been involved in protests. Chants of "Ashe! Power!" were also used in that context.

28 Public Affairs, "Message to the Campus Community about 'Occupy Cal,'" *Berkeley News*, November 10, 2011, http://news.berkeley.edu/2011/11/10/message-to-the-campus-community-about-occupy-cal/.

29 Linda Lye, "Police Violence on Peaceful Protesters Threatens the Health of Our Democracy," ACLU *Northern California*, November 22, 2011, https://www.aclunc.org/blog/police-violence-peaceful-protesters-threatens-health-our-democracy.

"this is a man's car!" For him, the sacredness of private property, symbolized by the red convertible in which Tim Wolfe rides, trumps the history of racial injustice that cs1950 seeks to bring to light. Arms outstretched like a basketball player on man-to-man defense, he shields Tim Wolfe's car from damage.

It is not only the car that the white spectators defend; they also protect white bodies from Black bodies. By linking arms, the white spectators take up the idea that white men are the most victimized in contemporary society due to racism by Black people against white people that those on the political left hypocritically refuse to acknowledge.[30] Conservative radio personalities including Sean Hannity and Glenn Beck, as well as the news service run by Andrew Breitbart, have devoted considerable attention to alleged acts of violence or intimidation perpetrated by Black people against white people, especially those connected to the Black Lives Matter movement.[31] Indeed, the white conservative response to this movement, expressed in the slogan "All Lives Matter" mirrors the parade spectators' chant of "M-I-Z/Z-O-U" in that it is an appeal to inclusivity that rejects evidence of discrimination against Black people.

The confrontation between lines of Black and white people with linked arms symbolizes the racialized, political polarization that has developed in the US over the past several years. While Black intellectuals such as Ta-Nehisi Coates point out the ways white people have robbed Black people throughout US history, Glenn Beck mocks the notion of white privilege and urges those who share his views to join "in peace, bind ourselves together and stand arm-in-arm."[32] When Donald Trump, then

30 For example, Daniel Greenfield, "It's Time to Call Out Black Racism," *Frontpage Mag,* August 5, 2015.

31 For example, Jason Howerton, "Black Lives Matter Mob Invades Dartmouth Library," *The Blaze,* November 16, 2015. Responses like this, by white people to Black allegations of racism brings to mind Lorraine Ryan's idea of "counter-memory of counter-memory," in this volume.

32 Ta-Nehisi Coates, "The Case for Reparations," *The Atlantic,* June 2014, https://www.theatlantic.com/magazine/archive/2014/06/the-case-for-reparations/361631/. Glenn Beck, "'These People Are Crazy': Glenn Reacts

a presidential candidate, declared, "I won't give up my micro-phone," after a Black Lives Matter protester disrupted a cam-paign event, he contested the narrative that Black protesters had been silenced by positioning himself as the one who was bravely speaking out.[33] In sum, the status of victim and perpetrator are unstable. The white spectators cast Tim Wolfe and his car as be-ing under attack just as the cs1950 protesters seek to remind the crowd of their vulnerability as Black people.

Yet the white people who link arms in front of Wolfe's car had other options. At 8:10, a white woman approaches and seeks per-mission to link arms with a protester. Four more people (some white, some apparently Latinx, including one pregnant woman) join the chain. It is notable that none of them wear Mizzou gear, although their actions seem to be spontaneous; "buying into" black and gold clothing is inversely correlated with solidarity with the protesters. These allies of cs1950 add to and change the meaning of the linked arms: white spectators are offered a choice between solidarity with or against the demonstrators.

The Video as a Polysemic Object

While the analyses I presented above are intended to break down the video into a series of signs, the video itself also func-tions as a sign. Its afterlife on the internet allows it to circulate indefinitely, accumulating meanings.

The meaning of this sign is contested by polarized groups of viewers whose process of semiosis is evidenced in the long string of written comments they have left. The video seems to function in two ways: to signify white annoyance with, disbe-lief at, and resentment of Black people's supposedly unfounded

---

to Shocking Video from the 2014 White Privilege Conference," *Glenn*, May 13, 2014.

33 Denis Slattery, "Black Lives Matter Protester Beaten and Kicked after Disrupting Donald Trump's Speech," *NY Daily News*, November 21, 2015, http://www.nydailynews.com/news/politics/black-lives-matter-protester-disrupts-donald-trump-article-1.2442688.

or hypocritical allegations of racism; and alternately, to signify Black and Black-allied sympathy with CS1950.

In the first vein, on November 8, 2015, the YouTube account "Brooke Hopkins" wrote, "What exactly is the issue? I am hearing a lot of angry yelling." In doing so, she questions whether the racism CS1950 seeks to bring to light is real or severe and suggests that the protesters are overreacting. In a similar way, on November 11th, the account "bigstudwithaguitar" described the protesters as "generally disgruntled black people being generally disgruntled... therefore, he's [Tim Wolfe's] racist." These commenters belittle the protesters rather than seeing them as a threat. They express fatigue at allegations of racism against white people.

Other observers see greater menaces. The account "Schlomo Shunn" responded to Brooke's question on November 10th: "... Of course, no mention of black-on-white violence, slurs, etc. No mention of black-only organization, classes, etc. No mention of how many protesters are affirmative-action quotazoids getting a free ride [...]." This commenter finds meaning beyond the protest itself, in a society that he sees as racist against white people. They have a timeline in their mind as well, yet it includes other milestones. This commenter also engages in a memory practice, thus drawing attention the fact that memory is always selective and not always reliable.

Both of these interpretations — the protest as a laughable annoyance, and as another brick in the wall of "Black supremacy" — are contested. On November 9th, the account "Becca Helen" responded to Brooke as well: "I suggest you actually LISTEN TO THEIR WORDS. Then, WALK A MILE IN THEIR SHOES." Becca's comments situate her as a non-Black ally of CS1950, as a person who might have linked arms with the protesters.

Some Black commenters took a more direct approach to white (mis)representations of the protest. On November 11th, the account "HVCAR PHOENIX" wrote, "What struggle do these kids have??? They act as if THEY are slaves... [...] what a joke... They will NEVER get anywhere or achieve anything blaming the past or other people for their problems........" On

November 11th, the account "toni bell" wrote, "HVACR PHOE-NIX We blame our past because IT CONSTANTLY messes with our future! Did you not listen to what they were saying?? There is still racism and discriminatory actions at this college as you can see the White people were more concerned with a dumb parade than the truth and facts the students where giving. Boy White privilege is a disease in this country! [...]." By using "we," "toni bell" inserts herself into CS1950's demonstration, link-ing arms with the protesters, while we can imagine "HVCAR PHOENIX" joining the white voices chanting over the protest-ers or the white bodies protecting Wolfe's car.

Discontinuity

We are left with these commenters' words, but we cannot access their visceral reactions as they watched the video. Their words are the only traces we have of their collective memories of race. As these comments and the video itself illustrate, many white people assign different meanings to race and racism than many Black people do. Yet this analysis is not only about cognition, but also about corporeality. Race is, as Narvaez would say, "sedi-mented" in all of our bodies.[34]

Despite watching the video many times, my own body's reac-tion has not been dulled. Without fail, when the white people link arms in front of Wolfe's car, the hair on the back of my neck stands up. I feel frozen in place and tears blur my vision. It is the embodied collective memory of white bystanders who wit-ness racial injustice and do nothing. I feel the history in which I am trapped and which is trapped in my body, the history that only partially escapes into the words on this page. It is too late to intervene.

But it is not too late to change the future. Trauma specialist Resmaa Menakem has explained how "white-body supremacy" affects people of all races, and has suggested that there are routes

---

34 Rafael F. Narvaez, *Embodied Collective Memory*.

to healing racial trauma through somatic practices.[35] I can offer no expertise in these practices, but I am convinced, after watching this video so many times, that collective memories involving race are so powerful that people cannot simply think their way out of them. Racist policies can and must change, and we need to use our full intellectual faculties to make that happen.[36] But if there is a space for discontinuity to erupt into the present, and for new, more just social structures to emerge, our bodies cannot be left behind.

35 Resmaa Menakemm, *My Grandmother's Hands: Racialized Trauma and the Pathway to Mending Our Hearts and Bodies* (Las Vegas: Central Recovery Press, 2017), 18.

36 Ibram X. Kendi, *How to Be and Anti-Racist* (London: One World, 2019).

Bibliography

"African American Vernacular English." *Portland State University,* 2020. https://www.pdx.edu/multicultural-topics-communication-sciences-disorders/african-american-vernacular-english-aave.

Baldwin, James. "Stranger in the Village." *Harper's Magazine,* October 1953.

Beck, Glenn. "'These People Are Crazy': Glenn Reacts to Shocking Video from the 2014 White Privilege Conference." *Glenn,* May 13, 2014.[37]

"Black Mizzou Players Say They'll Strike until President Tim Wolfe Resigns." *ESPN,* November 7, 2015. http://www.espn.com/college-football/story/_/id/14078494/missouri-tigers-football-players-strike-embattled-tim-wolfe-resigns.

Bowker, Geoffrey C. *Memory Practices in the Sciences.* Cambridge: MIT Press, 2005.

Brown, Ruth Nicole, Rozana Carducci, and Candace R. Kuby. *Disrupting Qualitative Inquiry: Possibilities and Tensions in Educational Research.* New York: Peter Lang, 2014.

Coates, Ta-Nehisi. "The Case for Reparations." *The Atlantic,* June 2014. https://www.theatlantic.com/magazine/archive/2014/06/the-case-for-reparations/361631/.

Concerned Student. "1839 Built on our Black Homecoming Parade Demonstration." *YouTube,* October 13, 2015. https://www.youtube.com/watch?v=u6zwnmlzZSQ.

Flewitt, Rosie, Regine Hampel, Mirjam Huack, and Lesley Lancaster. "What Are Multimodal Data and Transcription?" In *The Routledge Handbook of Multimodal Analysis,* edited by Carey Jewitt, 44–59. 2nd edition. New York: Routledge, 2014.

---

37 I do not include a URL to this article and other certain articles I reference in this chapter, because I do not want to direct traffic to these sites. I do not find these sources reputable, and they exhibit racist or racially-coded language. I cite the articles only to demonstrate that language is not my own.

Greenfield, Daniel. "It's Time to Call Out Black Racism." *Frontpage Mag,* August 5, 2015.

Guba, Egon G., and Yvonne S. Lincoln. "Competing Paradigms in Qualitative Research." In *The Landscape of Qualitative Research,* ed. Norman K. Denzin and Yvonna S. Lincoln. Thousand Oaks: Sage, 1994.

Howerton, Jason. "Black Lives Matter Mob Invades Dartmouth Library." *The Blaze,* November 16, 2015.

Jewitt, Carey. "An Introduction to Multimodality." In *The Routledge Handbook of Multimodal Analysis,* edited by Carey Jewitt, 15–30. 2nd edition. New York: Routledge, 2014.

Kendi, Ibram X. *How to Be an Anti-Racist.* London: One World, 2019.

Kress, Gunther. "What Is Mode?" In *The Routledge Handbook of Multimodal Analysis,* edited by Carey Jewitt, 60–75. 2nd edition. New York: Routledge, 2014.

Lye, Linda. "Police Violence on Peaceful Protesters Threatens the Health of Our Democracy." ACLU *Northern California,* November 22, 2011. https://www.aclunc.org/blog/police-violence-peaceful-protesters-threatens-health-our-democracy.

Menakem, Resmaa. *My Grandmother's Hands: Racialized Trauma and the Pathway to Mending Our Hearts and Bodies.* Las Vegas: Central Recovery Press, 2017.

Narvaez, Rafael F. "Embodiment, Collective Memory and Time." *Body & Society* 12, no. 3 (2006): 51–73. DOI: 10.1177/1357034X06067156.

———. *Embodied Collective Memory: The Making and Unmaking of Human Nature.* Lanham: University Press of America, 2013.

Pinnow, Rachel J. "An Ecology of Fear: Examining the Contradictory Surveillance Terrain Navigated by Mexican Youth in a U.S. Middle School." *Anthropology & Education Quarterly* 44, no. 3 (2013): 253–68. DOI: 10.1111/aeq.12033.

Public Affairs. "Message to the Campus Community about 'Occupy Cal.'" *Berkeley News,* November 10, 2011. http://

news.berkeley.edu/2011/11/10/message-to-the-campus-community-about-occupy-cal/.

Slattery, Denis. "Black Lives Matter Protester Beaten and Kicked after Disrupting Donald Trump's Speech." *NY Daily News,* November 21, 2015. http://www.nydailynews.com/news/politics/black-lives-matter-protester-disrupts-donald-trump-article-1.2442688.

"Student Enrolment Data." *University of Missouri,* 2016. http://ir.missouri.edu/EnrollmentData.html.

Vannini, Phillip. "Social Semiotics and Fieldwork: Methods and Analytics." *Qualitative Inquiry* 13, no. 1 (2007): 113–40. DOI: 10.1177/1077800406295625.

6

History

Alexandra Oeser

Roger Brubaker and Frederick Cooper published in 2000 a paper entitled "Beyond Identity."[1] Their conclusions on identity can be applied very efficiently to memory studies. To do this, we need first of all to remember that "memory studies" is everything but a coherent field and that national specificities, notably linked to language particularities persist, even if the profusion of the term has taken place in most of the western academic spheres. This article will specifically use the French debate to develop the link between the discussions on "identity" and those on "memory." The French debate is indeed somewhat specific for two reasons. First, The historians of nation-building, such as Reinhard Bendix (1964),[2] Karl Deutsch (1953),[3] Thomas Humphrey Marshall (1950),[4] published during the two decades following the Second World War, have never been translated into

1   Rogers Brubaker and Frederick Cooper, "Beyond Identity," *Theory and Society* 29 (2000): 1–47.

2   Reinhard Bendix, *Nation-building & Citizenship: Studies of Our Changing Social Order* (New York: John Wiley and Sons, 1964).

3   Karl Deutsch, *Nationalism and Social Communication: An Inquiry into the Foundations of Nationalism* (Cambridge: The Technological Press; New York: John Wiley and Sons, 1953).

4   Thomas Humphrey Marshall, *Citizenship and Social Class, and Other Essays* (Cambridge: Cambridge University Press, 1950).

French and a majority of French scholars are therefore not familiar with them. It was only at the end of the 1980s and during the 1990s that French historians and political sociologists discovered some of the newer literature in English on nations and nationalism.[5] Late and variable translations meant that the two academic contexts were marked by different, sometimes contradictory, debates.[6] Second, while the English-speaking world was busy discussing nations and nationalisms between the 1950s and 1990s, the French started discussing the concept of memory in the 1980s without the discussions around nation-building that were taking place in the literature in English. This meant that memory came to replace the notion of the nation in France to a certain extent, even if works on the nation continued to be produced, leading to the crystallization of certain uses of the concept of memory in a way that has not occurred in English-language works. Indeed, in France probably more than anywhere else, due to this specific editorial context and a certain closure of the French-intellectual field to English writing, the

---

5   The following generation from the 1980s and 1990s had to wait more than ten years before being imported into French political sociology and history. Benedict Anderson's classic text, *Imagined Communities* (London: Verso, 1983), was only translated into French in 1996. Roger Brubaker's *Nationalism Reframed: Nationhood and the National Question in the New Europe* (Cambridge: Cambridge University Press, 1996) still has yet to be translated; only his early book, *Citizenship and Nationhood in France and Germany* (Cambridge: Harvard University Press, 1992) has been translated into French in 1996. Ernest Gellner's work *Nations and Nationalism* (Oxford: Blackwell Publishers, 1983), was translated somewhat more quickly into French in 1989. Only the works of Eric Hobsbawm were fully translated within two years of their publication in English and imported into the French market in the late 1980s and early 1990s.

6   A well-documented example of this is what the Anglo-Saxon world calls "French Theory," which consists in reading a series of French authors, philosophers, sociologists, psychologists, and feminists together, where French academia considers them to be in fervent opposition to each other and impossible to read together or, even less, to consider as a coherent corpus of literature. François Cusset, *French Theory: How Foucault, Derrida, Deleuze, and Co. Transformed the Intellectual Life of the United States* (Minneapolis: University of Minnesota Press, 2008).

uses of the term memory have become unavoidably entwined with that of the nation.

The French case can thus be considered as an extreme case, which allows us to understand certain dangers implied in the use of the concept of memory, which might be more diffuse in the English-language literature.[7] I will thus expose the different ways in which the term "memory" has been used in France from the 1980s onward, the consequences it had in theoretical terms on the historical field, and the alternative terms that could replace the term "memory" in each of these very different cases, before explaining how I dealt with the problem in my own work.

Memory versus Everyday History: A Fight for Legitimacy

The debates on the differences between history and memory, between the "knowledge about the past" and the "identity stakes," are at the basis of the construction, during the 1980s in France, of a domain of study inside the historical discipline: that of "memory as history of history."[8] Gérard Noiriel has insisted upon the potential of this historical turn: to study no longer the past itself but the ways in which it is constructed, put into form, institutionalized and transmitted[9]. Thus, studying the "political uses of the past"[10] could reconcile French historical studies

---

7   Florence Weber, "Settings, Interactions and Things: A Plea for Multi-integrative Ethnography," *Ethnography* 2, no. 4 (December 2001): 475–99.

8   Pierre Nora, *Les lieux de mémoire* (Paris: Quarto Gallimard, 1997). In the last twenty years, memory studies have been constituted into its own scientific field, to a point that the American historian Alon Confino designs the notion of memory as "maybe the leading term in cultural history." Alon Confino, "Collective Memory and Cultural History: Problems of Method," *The American Historical Review* 102, no. 5 (December 1997): 1386. See also Alon Confino, "Telling about Germany: Narratives of Memory and Culture," *The Journal of Modern History* 76, no. 2 (June 2004): 398–416 and Alon Confino, "Introduction," *History & Memory* 17, no. 1–2 (Fall 2005): 5–11.

9   Gérard Noiriel, "Pour une approche subjectiviste du social," *Annales: Histoire, Sciences Sociales* 44, no. 6 (1989): 1452.

10 Jacques Revel and François Hartog, eds., *Les usages politiques du passé* (Paris: Editions de l'Ecole des Hautes Etudes en Sciences Sociales, 2001).

with comprehensive sociology from Max Weber to the English speaking sociology of interactionism developed notably by Herbert Mead, in the common analysis of representations of the past but also in taking into account *Erlebnis* (lived experience), which is at the center of questions about memory.

The debate is not new. The distinction between history and memory is as old as the birth of historical research in the West. Krzyzstof Pomian, a Franco-Polish historian publishing in French and Polish (he has very little been translated into English) is nevertheless cited in literature in English. He has shown that the separation between two different ways to evoke the past has taken place in the fifteenth and sixteenth centuries. A new way to apprehend the past is defined, reposing upon the mediate knowledge of the past, as the study of traces and not the direct perception: documents, monuments, images, or objects. The mediate knowledge of the past, in opposition to the immediate perception, becomes a legitimate way of doing history, even if other ways can be practiced in parallel. The consequence is a "redefinition of history, which is simultaneously separated from memory and from literature to be identified with the study of the past through the intermediary of sources."[11] This cognitive evolution, starting during the fifteenth century, will take more than three centuries and has marked not only a major, epistemological change of the status of history, it has also inverted the relation between memory and history: "it's the end of the superiority of memory over history, with the parallel ending of the superiority of the oral over the written."[12] Basing the work on traces, history becomes a (university) discipline, which is situated at the junction of human and social sciences but is keeping to be very heterogeneous in its practices.[13]

---

11 Krzysztof Pomian, "De l'histoire, partie de la mémoire, à la mémoire, objet d'histoire," in *Sur l'histoire* (Paris: Gallimard, 1999), 322. My translation.

12 Ibid.

13 Today, we could thus define, with Pomian, history as "heterogeneous cognitive practices ranging from traditional approaches to very pointed techniques, heterogeneous practices of styles of writing ranging from the most literary to the equations of an econometric model. [It is also] the re-

This transformation of history into a discipline of knowledge has had the effect "of the appearance of suspicion towards narrative sources, the accounts of participants or witnesses, which impose their points of view and their judgements and of which the truthfulness is never certain before they have been confronted the ones with the others and all with documents which have beforehand been submitted to critical investigation."[14] The distrust towards narrative sources has gone hand in hand with the triple, and disappointed, hope of history as a science: history had to renounce the old dream to be able to recount the past in a total or global way, to apprehend it in a purely descriptive manner, and finally to occupy a neutral and objective point of view. This triple deception has been accompanied, during the 1970s, by a return towards a more modest way of writing history and a revision of its ambitions.[15] That is also the period of a constructivist turn in the social sciences, criticizing, sometimes in a denunciatory posture, the essentialism of a series of notions, such as identity and tradition.[16]

From there, historians will rediscover, in a very different way, the oral sources, multiplied through the revolution of the media and the possibilities of registering voices of witnesses which were absent from the archives. The result has been an enlargement of the notion of the archive. This change is certainly also the result of a renewed dialogue between history and anthropology and/or ethnology and the tentative of some historians to

---

sult of a succession of a million years of sedimentations, each of which has left behind a series of questions, of procedures, of documents and monuments, and written works of historians. As a result, it is a superposition of these layers one upon the other, later layers modifying the significance, if not the appearance, of all the earlier ones, through a return-effect." Ibid., 331.

14 Ibid.

15 Jacques Revel, "Ressources narratives et connaissance historique," *Enquête* 1 (1995): 43.

16 For a critical review of the constructivist turn and its consequences on notions of "identity," see Martina Avanza and Gilles Laferté, "Dépasser la 'construction des identités'? Identification, image sociale, appartenance," *Genéses* 61, no. 4 (2005): 134–52.

give a voice and a right to talk to those without, *les sans voix.*[17] In Germany, this has given rise to the historical current of *Alltagsgeschichte* — history of the everyday. In Great Britain, it is oral historians who work towards the enlargement of the notion of history and impose critical reflections on the realm of historian's work. The discussion is simultaneously methodological and political. It enlarges the notion of the archives, notably to oral but also to juridical sources and that of legitimacy. History from below, in Italy and France the currents of micro-history, include popular, non-state events into the definition and practice of history. The research on the Nazi past can be considered as emblematic of this change of statue of certain sources: the distrust in the written archive, fabricated by the Nazi administration, is at the base for the demand of a rehabilitation of private and plural voices of the past, recollected, for example, through interviews.

At the same time, in France, Pierre Nora sets out to establish the notion of memory as distinct from history: "everything opposes them [the two terms]."[18] This theoretical distinction can be seen at best, as an alternative way to the micro- and everyday historians of including less legitimate sources into the work of historians, at worst as a backlash of precise exclusion of those alternative voices from the nobility of entering the realm of history. It is the latter effect that, probably involuntarily by its

---

17 On the dialogue between history and ethnology, see Hans Medick, "'Missionare im Ruderboot'? Ethnologische Erkenntnisweisen als Herausforderung an die Sozialgeschichte," in *Alltagsgeschichte: zur Rekonstruktion historischer Erfahrungen und Lebensweisen,* ed. Alf Lüdtke (Frankfurt: Campus Verlag, 1989), 48–84. The influence of this dialogue on the analysis of commemorations has been shown by Gerald Sider and Gavin Smith, "Introduction," in *Between History and Histories: The Making of Silences and Commemorations,* eds. Gerald Sider and Gavin Smith (Toronto: Toronto University Press, 1997), 3–28. See also David William Cohen, *The Combing of History* (Chicago: University of Chicago Press, 1994).

18 Pierre Nora, "Entre mémoire et histoire. La problématique des lieux," in *Les lieux de mémoire,* 24. Part of this monumental work was translated into English in 1996 by Arthur Goldhammer under the title "Realms of Memory: The Construction of the French Past." It gives English speakers access to forty-six of the 132 articles that made up the French edition.

author, has dominated French and international receptions of the "realms of memory." The rush for memory as a concept, in this context, has had as a side effect the effacement of works of everyday historians. The enormous effort to work toward an inclusion of plural voices into the writing of history is countered by the illusion that works on memory have precisely the same effect. Or, the opposite is true. The colossal project of the realms of memory is a return to writing an official and very legitimate "history of the history of France," and thereby, by introducing a new term, covering up the fact that the way history is written here is precisely what the historians of the everyday in Germany, the oral historians in Great Britain, and the microhistorians in Italy have tried to overcome. Instead, talking about the "silent voices" of oral or everyday history and of micro-history permits to turn to a series of works that have been very productive over the last forty years.

Memory as National Identity: The "Pierre Nora Project"

Pierre Nora has rallied a great part of the French historical community around his project. Seven volumes and more than 5000 pages published in the very prestigious *Bibliothèque illustrée des histoires* have been written by 130 historians, among them are microhistorians and social historians, which might be one of the reasons for its large consensus and international success. The impressive work accomplished and the passionate analysis of these official, political, and intellectual representations of the past are nevertheless implicitly creating an illusion: "The Republic," "The nation," and "The France" (even though in plural, Les France) are represented by their legitimate culture (from Pierre Larousse to Voltaire, Proust, and Hugo, passing the Marseillaise, the historical museum of Versailles and the Louvre, and, not to forget, the Annales), their legitimate institutions (Collège de France, Khâgne, Justice, the Bourbon Palace, classical textbooks, the "grands corps," the king, the state) and their buildings (Notre Dame de Paris, palaces of the Loire, Sacré-Coeur of

Montmartre, the tour Eiffel, the Pantheon, and even all of Paris),
middle-class professions (liberal professions, the bar, the notary,
the firm), legitimate individuals or "great men" (the great writ-
er, famous sayings, the soldier Chauvin, Proust, Charlemagne,
Jeanne d'Arc, Descartes), their political representations, their
realities created by the state (frontiers, regions, departments,
administration, statistics, archives, etc.). Some exceptions — the
article of Michèle Perrot on worker's lives, Gérard Noiriel's
work on French-foreigners, the one of the couple Ozouf on the
popular library of the third district of Paris (on a workers elite
but nevertheless on their reading practices, which can certainly
enter into "high culture"), and two sections, entitled, a little am-
biguously *roots* and *singularity* (where we can find some every
day, such as conversation, the coffeeshop, gastronomy, sayings,
myths and songs) do not balance the main impression. We are
here in front of a restricted, white, intellectual upper-middle-
class definition of high culture by the French historical profession, only rarely taking into account popular culture or folklore,
for example. Nora has realized a critical approach of this high
culture. All of the articles are conscious of the constructivist dimension of identity, of "the Nation," "the Republic," and "the
Frances" by these intellectuals, texts, monuments, and traces.
They enter into the mechanisms underpinning the creation of
unity and groups, feelings of belonging and otherness. Nevertheless, reuniting these critical "second-degree" histories on the
production of history and identity in seven volumes which will
represent France's *lieux de mémoire* contributes, in return, to the
production of history and identity described, and criticized, in
what has become itself a monument. Pierre Nora is aware of this
certainly unwanted effect of his critical history, as he himself
shows in the article concluding *Les Lieux de mémoire* in 1993,
while he had time — ten years — to observe the readings and effects caused by the first and second volumes. In the end, Nora
has managed to write a "history of France" in the "French style,"

from Michelet to Braudel,[19] without writing a history of France, or rather, by writing on the writing of the history of France, a brilliant double salto that assured him success within the historical profession, through collaboration with 130 historians, and beyond, and outside it in the larger public. Nevertheless, it had lasting effects on the uses of the term memory, which has become ineluctably entwined to that of the nation. In a way, the different national enterprises of Pierre Nora's *lieux de mémoire* have come to be a substitute for the much criticized notion of national identity.[20] But they have in no way resolved the problems caused by the latter notion.

In Germany, historiography took a different turn in the 1980s. The first study of popular, fascist memories in the Ruhr, by Lutz Niethammer, Alexander von Plato, and their research group was conducted by a group of historians practicing history of the everyday (*Alltagsgeschichte*).[21] For a long time, it was the only one exploring the shift from "official" to "popular" memories. It seems remarkable that this study, conducted at the same time as Pierre Nora's *Les Lieux de mémoire,* has encountered comparatively little lasting resonance among French or international

---

19 As Jacques Revel has put it, "[w]e have to admit: France (that is rather, French intellectuals) have a strange relation to their past: at the same time authoritarian and hesitating. Since the Middle Ages, the novel of the nation had a triple function: to affirm an identity, to grant a continuity, and to create a community of destiny." Jacques Revel, "Le fardeau de la mémoire: Histoire et mémoire dans la France d'aujourd'hui," in *Un parcours critique: Douze exercices d'histoire sociale* (Paris: Galaade Editions, 2006), 377.

20 The rapid internationalization of Nora's approach can be seen in the following texts, which all reproduce the same "realms of memory" model for various countries. See Étienne François and Hagen Schulze, *Deutsche Erinnerungsorte* (Munich: C.H. Beck, 2001); Martin Sabrow, *Erinnerungsorte der DDR* (Munich: C.H. Beck, 2009); Sonja Kmec, Benoit Majerus, Michel Margue, and Pit Peporte, eds., *Lieux de mémoire au Luxembourg: Usages passé et construction nationale* (Luxembourg: Editions Saint Paul, 2008); and Mario Isnenghi, *L'Italie par elle-même: Les lieux de mémoire italiens de 1848 à nos jours* (Paris: Editions Rue d'Ulm, 2006).

21 Lutz Niethammer and Alexander von Plato, eds., *Lebensgeschichte und Sozialkultur im Ruhrgebiet 1930–1960* (Berlin: Dietz Verlag, 1985).

historians. It is true that both studies follow opposite logics. The German historians are interested in popular narrative representations of the Nazi past among working families of the Ruhr, mainly relying on interviews. They also do not excessively use the term "memory" but mobilize the concept of the history of everyday lives and that of social culture. They thus situate their study within the larger project of everyday history — a project which has, in many important ways, contributed to the decentralization of history writing.[22]

The French historians, on the contrary, use the term "memory" to describe official representations of history. They write about state representations of multiple pasts which are incorporated or expressed in monuments, texts, and traces, fulfilling implicit political expectations, confirmed by the rapid internationalization of the approach and the capture by the political field of the notion of memory.

More recent European attempts to leave the territory of the nation in order to escape this linkage between memory and nation recall earlier attempts on post-national identities. Indeed, we have now the *lieux de mémoire* of Europe, of Antiquity, of the Middle Ages, even of Christianity.[23] But it is not by enlarging the unity of the territory from the nation to Europe or Christianity that the principal logic, which is that of identity, disappears. In this case, there is no viable alternative. The notion of memory does not replace the problematic inferred by the notion of national identity. We should drop both, memory and identity, and talk about the production, construction, or framing of the nation. This allows us to turn to more than half a century of works

22 Alf Lüdtke, *The History of Everyday Life: Reconstructing Historical Experiences and Ways of Life* (Princeton: Princeton University Press, 1995).

23 Prim den Boer, Heinz Durchhardt, Georg Kreis, and Wolfgang Schmale, *Europäische Erinnerungsorte* (Munich: C.H. Beck, 2012). See also Elke Stein-Hölkeskamp and Karl Joachim Hölkeskamp, eds., *Erinnerungsorte der Antike* (Munich: C.H. Beck, 2006) and Christoph Markschies and Hubert Wolf, eds., *Erinnerungsorte des Christentums* (Munich: C.H. Beck, 2010).

on nation and nationalism, left aside by those works on memory that try and tackle exactly the same questions.

Public Policies of Memory: A Screen to Materialist Stakes

The success of the concept of memory has led other disciplines to discuss it too. In France, it is particularly sociologists and political scientists who have taken up the notion and used it in their specific fields. Public policy specialists have also noted the fact that successive governments have adopted the term and integrated it into their discourses and practices. This demonstrates how the state and the government have appropriated the notion of memory for policy purposes. Certain scholars, mostly political scientists, have started to talk about public policies of memory, to underline the governmental intention and distance themselves from an overall hegemonic vision of a national collective memory.[24]

Paradoxically, however, these works show that when one uses public policy concepts to analyze memory policy, one finds diplomacy, finance, politics of international relations, but not memory[25]. Politicians seem to mobilize memory purely in order to underline and reinforce other policies. These might even sometimes be related to war, as in the case of the construction of the United States Holocaust Memorial Museum in Washington, DC. The history of this museum cannot be understood without taking into account the discussions within the political field in the US. At the time, President Carter was attempting to make a gesture towards the Jewish community at home, while pleading for the right of the Palestinians for a homeland, accepting the Palestinian Liberation Organization as a partner for peace talks,

---

24 Johann Michel, *Gouverner les mémoires: Les politiques mémorielles en France* (Paris: Presses Universitaires de France, 2010).

25 Sarah Gensburger, *Les justes de France: Politiques publiques de la mémoire* (Paris: Presses de Science Po, 2010).

and selling weapons to Saudi Arabia and Egypt in the context of the Israeli–Lebanese conflict.[26]

Beyond memory, we thus find other issues, particularly financial and economic, which are parallel and contemporaneous to the politics of representation, and which tend to be overlooked when we use the term politics of memory, placing the interest in discourses only. The use of the term memory can therefore sometimes be misleading rather than analytically productive. It can hide material stakes, by cloaking them in representations. In this case, it does not allow us to see the power relations behind the so-called public policies of memory. In fact, rather than memory, it would be more heuristic to talk about finance, economics, and public policy, which allows us to simultaneously analyze material stakes and representations.

Memory from Below: Reception, Appropriation, Practices.

Since the 1990s, in both France and Germany, the shift towards the study of popular representations of the past, which was initiated in Germany by the history of the everyday, had a greater echo in disciplines other than history. Moreover, it may not be a coincidence that in both countries these studies are not conducted by historians but rather by social psychologists, sociologists, and political scientists.[27] The separation of these two dif-

---

26 Edward Linenthal, *Preserving Memory: The Struggle to Create America's Holocaust Museum* (New York: Columbia University Press, 2001).

27 To cite just some examples, in Germany, see Harald Welzer, Robert Montau, and Christine Plaß, *"Was wir für böse Menschen sind!" Der Nationalsozialismus im Gespräch zwischen den Generationen* (Tübingen: edition diskord, 1997); Harald Welzer, Sabine Moller, and Karoline Tschuggnall, *"Opa war kein Nazi": Nationalsozialismus und Holocaust im Familiengedächtnis* (Frankfurt am Main: Fischer Taschenbuch Verlag, 2002); Michael Kohlstruck, *Zwischen Erinnerung und Geschichte: Der Nationalsozialismus und die jungen Deutschen* (Berlin: Metropol, 1997); Nina Leonhard, *Politik- und Geschichtsbewußtsein im Wandel: Die politische Bedeutung der nationalsozialistischen Vergangenheit im Verlauf von drei Generationen in Ost- und Westdeutschland* (Munich: LIT Verlag, 2002); Sabine Moller, *Vielfache Vergangenheit: Öffentliche Erinnerungskulturen und Familienerinnerungen an die NS-Zeit in Ostdeutschland* (Tübingen:

ferent ways of studying representations of the past — from above
and from below, centering on the political field or on every-day
representations, and uses of the past — has reinforced a separation on a theoretical level between what has been named an "official memory," or memory from above, and a "private (or family) memory," also sometimes referred to as "reception." Alon
Confino, in a review on the literature of memory and particularly on the work of Henri Rousso, has pointed out that "the
evolution of memory stands like a foundational story against
which reception is measured. The separate narratives thus assume levels of analysis and explanation: we must first construct
the evolution of memory in order to understand its' meaning as
revealed in reception. But this, of course, is an artificial separation, for the meaning of memories' evolution commingles with,
and is dependent on, the story of its reception."[28] This perspective raises multiple problems.

First, there is often a slippage that occurs from the official
production of memory to its reception and appropriation, which
involves the transfer of the inherent problems in the former to
the latter. Second, if we take Confino's statement seriously, we
have to admit that we cannot study the production of discourses
on the past without studying how intellectual and political pro-
ducers anticipate they will be received. This means we have to go
back to the principal conclusions of the sociology of reception
and cultural studies, notably advanced by Hirschman and Hall,
but also by historians of the everyday, and study the actors *from
below*.[29] We need to examine their hesitations, interactions, and
everyday worries, the ways they make sense of their lives, and

edition diskord, 2003). In France, see Marie-Claire Lavabre, *Le fil rouge:
Sociologie de la mémoire communiste* (Paris: Presse de la Fondation Nationale des Sciences Politiques, 1994).

28 Confino, "Collective Memory and Cultural History."

29 Albert O. Hirschman, *Exit, Voice, and Loyalty: Responses to Decline in
Firms, Organizations and States* (Cambridge: Harvard University Press,
1970). See also Stuart Hall, "Codage/décodage," *Réseaux* 12, no. 68 (1994):
27–39.

the information, culture, and knowledge they are confronted with.

These two ideas imply a third one. Indeed, once we know we cannot analyze production of history without also studying its appropriations, and once we know that memory seems a too ambiguous and imprecise term to describe what is produced, we then have to ask what is it exactly, that is being appropriated? It might be discourses on identity or the nation; it might be history, histories, or historical discourses; it might be public policies; it also might be political opinions, religion, or culture. All of these make sense in specific settings, be they peer groups, family, relations with institutions, or the political field.

Fourth, this separation between "production" and "reception," or between "memory from above" and "memory from below," has its own theoretical difficulties. It is itself based on another classic dichotomy between the public and the private, the official and the intimate. It reflects the ancient opposition between the written and the oral, by which what is official can be found in public institutions (e.g., political, scientific, scholarly, media) expressed in written form, whereas the private is seen as the sphere of the individual and/or the family and expressed orally. I would like to argue, following the long-standing demands of feminist and gender studies, that we must move beyond this binary opposition, that the public and the private, the official and the family, the written and the oral are interdependent and intricately connected, and that one cannot be understood without the other. This also influences the analysis of representations of the past. These forms coexist, they superpose and influence each other in different spaces, according to the social configurations that structure the uses of the past.

Indeed, what we are in fact debating when we discuss practices from below, and analyze forms of appropriations, is the question of legitimacy. Who has the right to define what belongs to history? When we use the term memory, we clearly avoid asking that central question: do historians have a monopoly on this definition, or does the profession interact with ordinary citizens, with non-historians or amateurs, in order to trace the limits of and within their profession?[30] Worse, by avoiding this question, we exclude non-professionals from the possibility of interacting with professionals and thus undermine forty years of effort to write history differently. Using the notions of histories, life-histories, or histories of the self instead of memory has opened up very productive avenues for research.[31]

Beyond Memory: Histories and Narratives

The American historian and anthropologist David William Cohen has developed a critique precisely on this point.[32] Cohen called for the practices by which history is produced to be analyzed in terms of "practices of legitimation": "in the *evalua-*

---

30 Sider and Smith have explicitly raised this question and coordinated a collection of articles on the problems posed by the question of legitimacy. Gerald Sider and Gavin Smith, eds. *Between History and Histories: The Making of Silences and Commemorations* (Toronto: Toronto University Press, 1997).

31 For histories, see ibid. For life histories, see Niethammer and von Plato, eds., *Lebensgeschichte und Sozialkultur im Ruhrgebiet 1930–1960*. For histories of the self, see Alban Bensa and Daniel Fabre, *Une histoire à soi: Figurations du passé et localités* (Paris: Editions de la Maison des Sciences de l'Homme, 2001).

32 He developed this in his position paper on the "production of history" presented at the fifth roundtable of the Anthropology and History Congress in Paris in July 1986. This paper has never been published, although it inspired the author's book *The Combing of History* and other publications, including David William Cohen, "Further Thoughts on the Production of History," in *Between History and Histories: The Making of Silences and Commemorations,* eds. Gerald Sider and Gavin Smith (Toronto: Toronto University Press, 1997), 300–310. One might wonder at the reasons for not publishing a paper which constituted the basis for all the papers of the roundtable brought together in the anthology of Sider and Smith, since it was used to write the call for papers for the roundtable and furthermore "photocopies have been widely circulated." The author, who criticizes the separation of the fields of professional and amateur production of history and "the ways in which academic practice disguises its very own organization of production," ("Further Thoughts on the Production of History," 301) is in fact actively contributing to the separation of disciplinary frontiers and to the occultation of the process of professional production of history by not publishing the paper which has caused so many discussions.

tion of productions of history both outside and inside the guild, claims to authority and priority may be challenged and debated through such questions as 'whose history?' or 'who has the right to speak?,'" raising questions that are also simultaneously debated in subaltern studies.[33] Reflections about the processes by which history is produced, by professionals or not, lead Gerald Sider and Gavin Smith to affirm that "we can neither privilege nor deny either a 'grand narrative history' or multiple specific histories. Yet it is not particularly useful simply to associate 'history' with 'large systems and large processes' and 'histories' with the specific and the particular — the ethnographic as it were. So, by invoking plural *histories,* we are suggesting that these histories emerge both within and against larger social processes — against 'history' — and also, in significant ways, against the local and the locally-known as well."[34] In order to understand the production of history, historians therefore have to know "what is locally known" and integrate it into, and consider it as part of, the "production of history." What Sider and Smith say about the relationship between "history" and multiple "histories" is just as true for what others have called "history" and "memory." It is their interplay in the process of producing history and what is considered to be part of history, which should interest us. The theoretical distinction between the two, which occurs automatically when we use the term memory, can thus obstruct the comprehension of the process of production of history.

This position is marginal, however, particularly in the French historical field, perhaps because historians feel the need to distinguish between professional and non-professional history. This leads them to defend the use of two separate terms to protect the historical profession as a science. Indeed, this serves not only to legitimize the professional status but also to ensure the quality of the production of history. The definition of his-

---

33 Cohen, "Further Thoughts on the Production of History," 302. See also Gayatri Chakravorty Spivak, "Can the Subaltern Speak? Speculations on Widow-sacrifice," *Wedge* 7/8 (Winter/Spring 1985): 120–30.

34 Sider and Smith, *Between History and Histories,* 12.

tory therefore depends on who formulates it. It differs between professionals and non-professionals. But the notion of memory homogenizes forms of appropriation by defining them solely by opposition to professional history. On the contrary, studying forms of appropriation of history can provide a micro-level reconstruction of the complexity of meanings that history and histories can represent in the everyday lives of ordinary people. Conversely, as though by mirror image, it can also reveal the force by which a narrow definition of history (as Western, written, and discovered through the mediation of traces of the past) is imposed, and its consequences for those whose practices do not correspond to this definition. The study of forms of appropriation that are neither foreseen nor intended by historians or by institutions can thus mirror professional rules and norms involved in the production of history, which constitutes an important, if not the most important, pillar of legitimate culture. The use of histories allows us to reconstruct the link between professional historians and other social spheres, such as politics, school, work, and family, while taking into account the power relations at work in these spaces.

Constructing Alternatives

This approach was further developed in a collective book on family (hi)stories.[35] In this book, we chose to avoid the use of memory as a concept, because it did not satisfactorily respond to our question about the ways in which (hi)stories of the past are passed on within a kin group. We thus turned to the notions of histories and of narrative (récit). The latter has its own (also problematic) trajectory but has not experienced the "success" and corresponding dilution of meaning that the term memory has. Our central argument, in challenging the utility of Halbwachs's notion of collective memory, is that of the existence

---

35 Solène Billaud, Sibylle Gollac, Alexandra Oeser, and Julie Pagis, *Histoires de famille: Les récits du passé dans la parenté contemporaine* (Paris: Editions de la rue d'Ulm, 2015).

of a group, or collective, that he takes for granted. Yet the central assumption that the group exists has never provoked much controversy among those studying Halbwachs — because if we doubt the existence of a group, how can we apply the concept of memory without fundamentally betraying Halbwachs's central project? However, British anthropology of kinship has long since questioned the definition of a group in the case of families. They can form a group, but they can also form a network, which we have to look upon from the perspective of the individual, and which will change when we change our entry point (ego).[36] I therefore chose to move away from the notion of collective memory in order to focus on the way individuals move between families, school, and peer groups as they appropriate the past.

To conclude: After the French publication of *When Do We Talk about Hitler?* my research continued in this vein, confirming my decision to not take up the concept of memory, but rather to talk about forms of appropriation of history.[37] Indeed, many uses of the notion of memory have a tendency to blind us to the very subject (history transmission) we want to study; it refers to concepts which are just as criticized and problematic (identity, nation); it underlines a rigid separation between historians and other institutions; it has a tendency to essentialize groups, and it renders important parts of the processes of production of history (such as finance, economics, kin relations, historical practices) and the very functioning of their power relations invisible. If it were not for its impressive political success, involving funding for research positions, post-docs, doctoral studies, research programs, even whole research institutes, we may have

36 Alexandra Oeser and Sibylle Gollac, "Comparing Family Memories in France and Germany: The Production of History(ies) within and through Kin Relations," *Journal of Comparative Family Studies* 45, no. 3 (2011): 385–98.

37 Alexandra Oeser, *Enseigner Hitler: Les adolescents allemands face au passé nazi en Allemagne: Interprétations, appropriations et usages de l'histoire* (Paris: Editions de la Maison des Sciences de l'Homme, 2010). The English version was published under the title *"When Will We Talk about Hitler?" German Students and the Nazi Past* (New York: Berghahn Books, 2019).

long since agreed to leave the term to politicians and profane users and find a scientifically more heuristic alternatives (in the plural, varying with their specific use and context) for it. These alternatives would also allow us to stop pretending that what we are analyzing is new, just because we use a "new" term — memory — to designate it. It would allow us to build upon existing works and take into account highly productive debates on identity, nation, history, and everyday life.

Bibliography

Anderson, Benedict. *Imagined Communities.* London: Verso, 1983.

Avanza, Martina, and Gilles Laferté. "Dépasser la 'construction des identités'? Identification, image sociale, appartenance." *Genèses* 4, no. 61 (2005): 134–52. DOI: 10.3917/gen.061.0134.

Bendix, Reinhard. *Nation-building & Citizenship: Studies of Our Changing Social Order.* New York: John Wiley and Sons, 1964.

Bensa, Alban, and Daniel Fabre. *Une histoire à soi: Figurations du passé et localités.* Paris: Editions de la Maison des Sciences de l'Homme, 2001.

Billaud, Solène, Sibylle Gollac, Alexandra Oeser, and Julie Pagis, eds. *Histoires de famille: Les récits du passé dans la parenté contemporaine.* Paris: Editions de la rue d'Ulm, 2015.

Brubaker, Rogers, and Frederick Cooper. "Beyond Identity." *Theory and Society* 29 (2000): 1–47. DOI: 10.1023/A:1007068714468.

———. *Citizenship and Nationhood in France and Germany.* Cambridge: Harvard University Press, 1992.

———. *Nationalism Reframed: Nationhood and the National Question in the New Europe.* Cambridge: Cambridge University Press, 1996.

Cohen, David William. "Further Thoughts on the Production of History." In *Between History and Histories: The Making of Silences and Commemorations,* edited by Gerald Sider and Gavin Smith, 300–310. Toronto: Toronto University Press, 1997.

———. *The Combing of History.* Chicago: University of Chicago Press, 1994.

Confino, Alon. "Collective Memory and Cultural History: Problems of Method." *The American Historical Review* 102, no. 5 (December 1997): 1386–1403. DOI: 10.1086/ahr/102.5.1386.

———. "Introduction." *History & Memory: Studies in Representation of the Past* 17, no. 1–2 (Fall 2005): 5–11.

———. "Telling about Germany: Narratives of Memory and Culture." *The Journal of Modern History* 76, no. 2 (June 2004): 398–416. DOI: 10.1086/422934.

Cusset, François. *French Theory: How Foucault, Derrida, Deleuze, & Co. Transformed the Intellectual Life of the United States.* Minneapolis: University of Minnesota Press, 2008.

den Boer, Prim, Heinz Durchhardt, Georg Kreis, and Wolfgang Schmale, eds. *Europäische Erinnerungsorte,* Vol. 3: *Europa und die Welt.* Munich: Oldenbourg Verlag, 2012.

Deutsch, Karl. *Nationalism and Social Communication: An Inquiry into the Foundations of Nationalism.* Cambridge: The Technological Press; New York: John Wiley and Sons, 1953.

François, Étienne, and Hagen Schulze. *Deutsche Erinnerungsorte.* Vol. 3. Munich: Verlag C.H. Beck, 2001.

Gellner, Ernest. *Nations and Nationalism.* Oxford: Blackwell Publishers, 1983.

Gensburger, Sarah. *Les justes de France: Politiques publiques de la mémoire.* Paris: Presses de Science Po, 2010.

Hall, Stuart. "Codage/décodage." *Réseaux* 12, no. 68 (1994): 27–39.

Hirschman, Albert O. *Exit, Voice, and Loyalty: Responses to Decline in Firms, Organizations and States.* Cambridge: Harvard University Press, 1970.

Isnenghi, Mario. *L'Italie par elle-même: Les lieux de mémoire italiens de 1848 à nos jours.* Paris: Editions Rue d'Ulm, 2006.

Kmec, Sonja, Benoît Majerus, Michel Margue, and Pit Peporte, eds. *Lieux de mémoire au Luxembourg: Usages passé et construction nationale.* Luxemburg: Editions Saint Paul, 2007.

Kohlstruck, Michael. *Zwischen Erinnerung und Geschichte: Der Nationalsozialismus und die jungen Deutschen.* Berlin: Metropol, 1997.

Lavabre, Marie-Claire. *Le fil rouge: Sociologie de la mémoire communiste*. Paris: Presse de la Fondation Nationale des Sciences Politiques, 1994.

Leonhard, Nina. *Politik- und Geschichtsbewußtsein im Wandel: Die politische Bedeutung der nationalsozialistischen Vergangenheit im Verlauf von drei Generationen in Ost- und Westdeutschland*. Munich: LIT Verlag, 2002.

Linenthal, Edward. *Preserving Memory: The Struggle to Create America's Holocaust Museum*. New York: Columbia University Press, 2001.

Lüdtke, Alf. *The History of Everyday Life: Reconstructing Historical Experiences and Ways of Life*. Translated by William Templer. Princeton: Princeton University Press, 1995.

Marshall, Thomas Humphrey. *Citizenship and Social Class, And other Essays*. Cambridge: Cambridge University Press, 1950.

Markschies, Christoph, and Hubert Wolf, eds. *Erinnerungsorte des Christentums*. Munich: C.H. Beck, 2010.

Medick, Hans. "'Missionare im Ruderboot'? Ethnologische Erkenntnisweisen als Herausforderung an die Sozialgeschichte." In *Alltagsgeschichte: zur Rekonstruktion historischer Erfahrungen und Lebensweisen*, edited by Alf Lüdtke, 48–84. Frankfurt am Main: Campus Verlag, 1989.

Michel, Johann. *Gouverner les mémoires: Les politiques mémorielles en France*. Paris: Presses Universitaires de France, 2010.

Moller, Sabine. *Vielfache Vergangenheit: Öffentliche Erinnerungskulturen und Familienerinnerungen an die NS-Zeit in Ostdeutschland*. Tübingen: edition diskord, 2003.

Niethammer, Lutz, and Alexander von Plato, eds. *Lebensgeschichte und Sozialkultur im Ruhrgebiet 1930–1960*. 3 Vols. Berlin: Dietz Verlag, 1985.

Noiriel, Gérard. "Pour une approche subjectiviste du social." *Annales: Histoire, Sciences Sociales* 44, no. 6 (1989): 1435–59. DOI: 10.3406/ahess.1989.283663.

Nora, Pierre. *Les lieux de mémoire*. 7 vols. Paris: Gallimard, 1984–1993.

———. *Les lieux de mémoire*. Paris: Quarto Gallimard, 1997.

———. *Realms of Memory: The Construction of the French Past*. Translated by Arthur Goldhammer. New York, Columbia University Press, 1996.

Oeser, Alexandra. *Enseigner Hitler: Les adolescents allemands face au passé nazi en Allemagne: Interprétations, appropriations et usages de l'histoire*. Paris: Editions de la Maison des Sciences de l'Homme, 2010.

———. *"When Will We Talk about Hitler?" German Students and the Nazi Past*. New York: Berghahn Books, 2019.

Oeser, Alexandra, and Sibylle Gollac. "Comparing Family Memories in France and Germany: The Production of History(ies) within and through Kin Relations." *Journal of Comparative Family Studies* 45, no. 3 (2011): 385–98. DOI: 10.3138/jcfs.42.3.385.

Pomian, Krzysztof. "De l'histoire, partie de la mémoire, à la mémoire, objet d'histoire." In *Sur l'histoire,* 263–332. Paris: Gallimard, 1999.

Revel, Jacques. "Le fardeau de la mémoire: Histoire et mémoire dans la France d'aujourd'hui." In *Un parcours critique: Douze exercices d'histoire sociale,* 371–89. Paris: Galaade Editions, 2007.

———. "Ressources narratives et connaissance historique." *Enquête* 1 (1995): 43–70. DOI: 10.4000/enquete.262.

Revel, Jacques, and François Hartog, eds. *Les usages politiques du passé*. Paris: Editions de l'Ecole des Hautes Etudes en Sciences Sociales, 2001.

Sabrow, Martin. *Erinnerungsorte der DDR*. Munich: C.H. Beck, 2009.

Sider, Gerald, and Gavin Smith. "Introduction." In *Between History and Histories: The Making of Silences and Commemorations,* edited by Gerald Sider and Gavin Smith, 3–28. Toronto: Toronto University Press, 1997.

Sider, Gerald, and Gavin Smith, eds. *Between History and Histories: The Making of Silences and Commemorations.* Toronto: Toronto University Press, 1997.

Spivak, Gayatri Chakravorty. "Can the Subaltern Speak? Speculations on Widow-sacrifice." *Wedge* 7/8 (Winter/Spring 1985): 120–30.

Stein-Hölkeskamp, Elke, and Karl Joachim Hölkeskamp, eds. *Erinnerungsorte der Antike: Die römische Welt.* Munich: C.H. Beck, 2006.

Weber, Florence. "Settings, Interactions and Things: A Plea for Multi-integrative Ethnography." *Ethnography* 2, no. 4 (December 2001): 475–99. DOI: 10.1177/146613801002004002.

Welzer, Harald, Sabine Moller, and Karoline Tschuggnall. *'Opa war kein Nazi': Nationalsozialismus und Holocaust im Familiengedächtnis.* Frankfurt am Main: Fischer Taschenbuch Verlag, 2002.

Welzer, Harald, Robert Montau, and Christine Plaß. *'Was wir für böse Menschen sind!' Der Nationalsozialismus im Gespräch zwischen den Generationen.* Tübingen: edition diskord, 1997.

7

Questions

Elizabeth Anderson Worden

While studying history teachers in Republic of Moldova, I discovered that the inclusion of certain terms, such as "Soviet," in my interview questions led to answers with familiar tropes describing the country's communist past. When I asked the same questions without including "Soviet" or a related term, an interviewee would give very a different answer, often not alluding to communism at all. In a related example, my recent work in Northern Ireland revealed that some teachers were acutely aware of how they should talk about their past to their students and to a visiting researcher, which was likely different from their "real" views. One teacher even joked that he would "ham it up" for me in discussing "The Troubles" in Northern Ireland because I was visiting from America, with the supposition being that I expected him to have a particular bias based on his cultural identity.

These anecdotes highlight challenges that researchers face in understanding how memory practices influence individual behavior. How does a researcher ask questions in a way that avoids trite or manufactured answers or avoids magnifying a stereotype of the past that might not matter to an individual? How might the physical presence of a researcher act as a trigger for specific recollections? How does a researcher determine which memories have salience in everyday life? How might the performance of memory in the classroom, especially for an outside researcher, obscure the ways in which other memories shape teaching and learning?

To answer some of these questions, I propose that researchers take a holistic approach to understanding memory practices and reflect upon their own presence in the environment. The complexity and relevance of social memory might not be found only by focusing on specific historical events or periods, such as the Soviet Era or The Troubles. Social memory might be ahistorical and could be found in rituals, names, symbols, and even interior design. In Moldova, for example, uncovering the teachers' social memory and memory practices came from asking teachers about themselves and considering these discussions in light of the school environment, their classroom practice, their place in the school hierarchy and society, and their everyday reality. In this chapter, I aim to advance the methods used to investigate memory practices and begin a robust discussion about the challenges researchers encounter in moving beyond what I call the "expected past."

Understanding Social Memory and Memory Practices

A vast range of scholars have studied the concept of "social memory," or "collective memory," and have often "seen it as involving particular sets of practices like commemoration and monument building and general forms like tradition, myth or identity. [These scholars] have approached it from sociology, history, literary criticism, anthropology, psychology, art history, and political science among other disciplines."[1] In a broad sense, social memory is made up of the ways in which a group remembers a shared past. Yet it is much more complex than this simple definition because person can recall events and feelings from a century ago, even though he or she did not personally experi-

---

1   Jeffrey K. Olick and Joyce Robbins, "Social Memory Studies: From 'Collective Memory' to the Historical Sociology of Mnemonic Practices," *Annual Review of Sociology* 24 (1998): 106.

ence them. Memories of this sort are not recalled from some nook of the brain but are created and shaped by external social structures.[2] It is in society that people acquire, recall, recognize, and localize their memories.[3] Any given society, says Halbwachs, may have a vast array of collective memories, through families, churches, associations, social classes, and so forth.[4] Individuals, not groups, maintain the memories, but the group provides context and meaning for these memories to be maintained and constructed over long periods of time. As a product of society, social memory reveals more about the present than it does about the past.[5] Social memory also shapes present-day identities by influencing who and what we are as a nation, a community, a family, or any other of the innumerable social arrangements and groups to which we belong.[6] Memory also reflects society's aspirations for the future. It is "both a mirror and a lamp — a model of and a model for society."[7] Memory helps an individual locate themselves in the past, present, and future.

Understanding social memory in the context of society also requires us to understand memory as a process and a practice. Memory is more than just a thing. Public monuments, museums, and textbooks might reflect a society's shared memory, for example, a war memorial that celebrates a nation's victory or defeat. In isolation, however, these memorials do not capture how that memory informs and shapes social life because we would not know the value that individuals bestow on them. Anthropologist Margaret Paxson explains, "[o]ver time, the characteristics of memory transmission, preservation, and function have come to be seen as part of the dimension of broader social phe-

2   Maurice Halbwachs, cited in Margaret Paxson, *Solovyovo: The Story of Memory in a Russian Village* (Bloomington: Indiana University Press, 2005), 14.

3   Maurice Halbwachs, *On Collective Memory* (Chicago: University of Chicago Press, 1992).

4   Ibid., 46–51.

5   Ibid.

6   Olick and Robbins, "Social Memory Studies," 111.

7   Barry Schwartz, cited in ibid., 124.

nomena: it is now understood that *we recollect when and where we perform other social acts* — in ritual, narrative, language, religious practice, and the details of social and economic organization. [...] It takes place in the present: in its practices, it informs us of the social, political, ideological, and symbolic landscapes of today."[8]

Sites of Memory

Public (i.e., state-sponsored) schools are the focus of my work but my aim is to encourage the study of memory across actors and social institutions. How might social memory affect the decisions of a local government? or influence the outreach agenda of a church? How might it encourage citizen groups to protest or not? or guide university officials in making decisions about controversial events on campus? My work on schools and teachers could provide a helpful template for these types of investigations.

Returning to my focus here on schools, governments, consciously or not, are concerned with social memory because the national imaginings, myths, and heroes that form the basis for the nation also become the substance of social memory. These are reinforced and transmitted through official and government-supported narratives, such as textbooks. Historian James E. Young notes, "[i]f part of the state's aim, therefore, is to create a sense of shared values and ideals, then it will also be the state's aim to create a sense of common memory, as foundation for unified polis."[9] Public schools provide an incubator for developing this common memory, because schools are one of the state's primary vehicles for the creation of citizens. Schools also reflect social memory — who and what a society wishes to remember. Yet unlike other public places, such as memorials or museums, schools are not static spaces. They are busy places filled with stu-

---

8   Paxson, *Solovyovo*, 14.

9   James E. Young, *The Texture of Memory: Holocaust Memorials and Meaning* (New Haven: Yale University Press, 1993), 6.

dents, teachers, and administrators, who constantly create and recreate what happens inside.

For teachers in these schools, social memory is practiced in teaching, telling stories, and talking about the nation or other collective identities. By studying social memory as a practice, one can avoid exaggerating its importance. In theory, a history textbook reflects a nation's memory through its depiction of historical events and personages. But the text might or might not reflect how citizens actually recall their past or think of themselves. Studying only the textbook's portrayal of social memory might reflect how a state *would like* the nation to be depicted rather than how the nation is in fact perceived by its citizens. The memory practices that take place in individuals' everyday lives reveal which memories are salient, have meaning, and influence citizens' actions and thinking. For some, practices of social memory might be considered as "culture" or "identity." But these concepts, unlike social memory, do not adequately capture the act of remembering that is invoked when individuals talk about themselves.

The Case Studies: Moldova and Northern Ireland

For this chapter, I draw primarily from a project in the Republic of Moldova that I began in 2003 and finished in 2013.[10] I also draw from a more recent and ongoing project that I have begun in Northern Ireland. Although geographically and economically diverse, both of these societies have undergone social, political, or economic transitions in the past two and half decades, and both societies grapple with questions of identity and belonging. The Republic of Moldova is a post-Soviet state located between Romania and Ukraine with a population of approximately three-and-a-half million people. Since independence in 1991, the Moldovan government has struggled to foster economic and political development — national identity remains contested in

---

10 Elizabeth Anderson Worden, *National Identity and Educational Reform: Contested Classrooms* (New York: Routledge, 2014).

Moldova with disagreement about whom and what is a Moldovan. During eight months of field work in 2003, 2004, and 2008, I collected seventy-seven unique interviews with education actors and conducted school observations.

Like Moldova, Northern Ireland, which is part of the United Kingdom, has also undergone a transition. The Good Friday Agreement in 1998 ended over thirty years of a civil conflict referred to as "The Troubles." Though commonly perceived as a conflict between Protestants and Catholics because of the strong sectarian divisions, it was political and rested on the question of independence with Nationalists and Republicans, who are largely Catholic, supporting unification with the Republic of Ireland and Unionists and Loyalists, who are largely Protestant, supporting allegiance with the UK. The Troubles claimed over 3,500 lives and, despite the 1998 accords, social stability remains tenuous today. Northern Irish society remains deeply divided today, best exemplified by the fact that over ninety-five percent of school children attend separate schools based on their religion or "tradition." In Northern Ireland, my project is still ongoing, though I have conducted thirty-two interviews with a range of education actors and conducted school observations in 2012, 2014, 2015, 2017 and 2018. In total, I've spent approximately eight months living in Northern Ireland thus far.

Where Do We Find Memory?

Drawing from my field work, I propose that there are two methodological concerns when investigating social memory in schools. The first concern relates to the actual words, terms, and/or references that a researcher employs during interviews and discussions. As noted above, certain words and/or researcher might act as triggers for which an interviewee will recall the expected past — that is, the socially acceptable way to describe the past. The second concern regards the need for researchers to move beyond the confines of an interview or one's defined research boundary or scope (e.g., classroom observation or document analysis and so forth) in understanding why memories persist and are important to individuals.

Moving Beyond the Expected Past

Memories can be filtered and asking a "memory question" might lead to answers that are socially acceptable but might not reveal all an individual's feelings about the past.[11] This affirms Lather's concerns with questions about methods raised by poststructuralism: "[h]ow do we frame meaning possibilities rather than close them in working with empirical data?"[12] In the Moldovan case, I inadvertently closed memories by the term "Soviet." I discovered this almost by accident and it is worth elaborating upon here. One summer afternoon, Ana, a history teacher from central Moldova, and I went to visit her parents in the village where she grew up. Along the village's main street, we passed by Ana's elementary school, along which a Soviet-era mural ran the length of one exterior wall. The mural was crumbling along the edges, but the colors were still vibrant. Among other images, the mural depicted girls studying, practicing ballet, and looking through a microscope. Several of the girls were wearing red kerchiefs from the young pioneers. Ana reminisced on her school days as we looked at the mural. She laughed about how her strict parents would not allow her to go school dances or stay out late, so she played volleyball instead. Her volleyball team had a wonderful time as they travelled all over Soviet Moldavia. She still plays volleyball today. She described her favorite teacher who was charismatic and encouraging, and she told me

---

11 Here I borrow from sociologist Jon Fox who studies the ways in which individuals create and recreate national identity "from below" — i.e., from non-elite actors. In discussing research methods for studying ethnicity and nationality, Fox argues that one should not ask "an ethnic question" because the interviewer will get "an ethnic answer" that may or may not reflect an individual's true feelings about identity. Jon Fox, email correspondence, February 2005.

12 Patti Lather, "Critical Frames in Educational Research: Feminist and Poststructural Perspectives," *Theory into Practice* 31, no. 2 (1992): 95.

about studying archaeology at university and visiting St. Petersburg as a young adult.

I was surprised by these warm memories because I had previously interviewed Ana about her school experience. This was our exchange:

EAW: Tell me about school during the Soviet period. And what were the history lessons like?

Ana: In the Soviet period, history was taught differently from how it is taught now. First, history was taught from the point of view of the communist party, of course. It was a very ideological history. Teachers did not have the possibility to change something. It was impossible to think freely, impossible to even learn to think freely. Thus, it was politicized and idealized.

With reference to "Soviet," Ana recalls a time lacking in freedom. Yet when asked about school in general, Ana had a warmer reaction. After being struck by these differing memories, I returned to all of my interviews and discovered that the mention of "Soviet" or "communism" triggered a certain type of memory — a memory of the expected past. The following excerpts are from teachers who attended high school during the time of the Soviet Union:

EAW: Did you go to school during the communist period? Can you think of anything you do currently in your classroom that reminds you of your teachers?

Nicu: We have to keep one thing in mind that our predecessors — that is our history teachers — did not have the right to talk like we do nowadays. We had a totalitarian regime back then. It was prohibited to speak freely. Now it's much more open and free.

In this interview, I forgot to include "communist period" in the question:

EAW: Can you think of anything you do currently in your classroom that reminds you of your teachers?

Liliana: Back when I started my career and also throughout my career, some of the best examples of teaching material from my teachers stuck out, such as my history teachers or my biology teachers. What I remember most is the attitude they had towards students, towards me as a student, the pace of work they used during class, and the motivation strategies they employed with students. This is what I took over from them during difficult times or when I was confronted with a controversial situation with my students.

Again, when I forgot to mention "communist period":

EAW: Can you think of anything that you do currently in classes that reminds you of your teachers?

Cristina: When it was apparent that the class bored or tired, my favorite teacher made a joke to bring the students back to our history lesson. That I took from my teacher — to break up the lesson for children with a joke or sometimes I'll talk about a historical personality that is not in the lesson plan.

Lilliana and Cristina, who both teach in Chișinau and grew up during the USSR, answer the question with regard to pedagogy and do not mention the tropes, such as "totalitarian" or "could not speak freely," that Ana and Nicu used. The terms "Soviet" or "communist" bring the interviewees into a discursive space — a conversational space where interviewees consciously recall events in a way that is rational or socially acceptable (i.e., knowing that the Soviet period was a bad time and therefore recalling more negative memories).

For a few, the mention of "Soviet" did not necessarily trigger negative memories. Tudor, a historian who was born in 1937, said that "for a man of a certain age," like himself, the Soviet schools "were superior." While interviewing him in 2004, he noted that his positive views were "unpopular today" but said this is how he feels about the Soviet past. He remembers that pupils were disciplined and serious. Rodica, a teacher in southern Moldova and nearly thirty years younger than Tudor, remarked that education really depended upon the teacher. She recalled, "Soviet education was an informative education" and that the lessons "were less interactive" than today but it "depended upon the teacher and which methods she used." She considers herself lucky because she had good teachers. Vlad, a history teacher who has been teaching for thirty years, had mixed feelings about teaching in the Soviet period. He described, "[it] was not interactive, it was a passive process, where someone talks, and someone receives the information." Yet Vlad thought that Soviet textbooks were of better quality than those today. He uses the Soviet books when he is preparing his lessons for his current students. Tudor, Rodica, and Vlad were exceptional in my sample. Other teachers might have also had positive feelings or memories about the Soviet period but were less willing to admit them because such views are "unpopular today." Teachers, consciously or not, filtered their memories in filtered in describing the past regime.

Learning from my Moldovan experience, I purposefully did not ask about The Troubles during any of my Northern Irish interviews. Yet, The Troubles came up in every single interview. Moreover, at least two interviewees made reference to the performative aspect of talking about The Troubles. Patrick, a teacher at a prestigious Catholic school, made a joke to his class that he should "ham it up" for me. As if stepping into a clichéd role of a nationalist, he asked his class in a jovial voice: "Should we settle the unfinished business here for Elizabeth? Should we tell her how it is?" Patrick made light of what he thought I expected to him to be, a nationalist who yearned for freedom from the UK wore a Claddagh ring, and drank Guinness. And yet many of his stories throughout our interview and subsequent conversations were in line with this stereotype: he talked about "not if but when" Northern Ireland is reunified with Ireland, about his father who was an Irish language teacher, and about growing up during The Troubles. Within the first ten minutes of her interview, Frances told me in joking tone that "she was a child of The Troubles" and that I could ask her anything. But before I could ask her anything, she began a monologue of stories about the British soldiers raiding her childhood home in a Catholic neighborhood, of her cousins who were in the Irish Republican Army (IRA), and of losing friends to the conflict. Her remarks squared with the images that I had of The Troubles, gleaned from historical photographs, books, and film. Despite their joking about performing specific roles, Patrick and Frances filled these roles and told stories of the expected past.

Patrick's narrow role was subsurface and yet abundantly evident. Were these stories for me? Were they for their audience of students who were from the same community and might need or even demand the expected past? Were these stories told to maintain a comfortable and expected relationship? Last, were these stories necessary to establish and maintain trust between the teacher and students, a trust that would be needed for discussing difficult or sensitive classroom topics later?

How Do We Study Memory?

Moving Beyond Interview Transcripts to Understand Why Social Memory Persists

Scholarship on Moldovan identity tends to be framed in ethnic terms.[13] Yet, the ways in which Moldovans describe their country and the people of their country often transcend ethnic

---

13 For more on Moldovan national identity, see Matthew H. Ciscel, *The Language of the Moldovans: Romania, Russia, and Identity in an Ex-Soviet Republic* (Lanham: Lexington Books, 2007); Monica Heintz, ed., *Weak State, Uncertain Citizenship: Moldova* (Frankfurt am Main: Peter Lang, 2008); Charles King, *The Moldovans: Romania, Russia, and the Politics of Culture* (Stanford: Hoover Institution Press, 2000).

categories. In 2008, I asked thirty-five interviewees to describe "Moldova and the people of Moldova," and only two of them incorporated ethnicity into their answers. But there was wide agreement among the interviewees on abiding characteristics of *all* Moldovans, with adjectives such as "hospitable," "submissive," and "patient" being the most commonly used. Government officials, historians, teachers, and students alike described Moldovans as being "obedient and submissive to foreigners" and "used to putting up with things." In the words of one interviewee, Moldovans have "a high level of education and training but our psychology still carries many residual elements of a patriarchal society." They saw continuity between their past experiences and their present realities and between their lives and those of their parents and grandparents.

Moldova is an independent and democratic country, but many of its citizens still perceive of themselves as an occupied people, occupied by a neglectful and temporary state.[14] I define this as social memory, and these memories remain despite overt messages from the government and media asserting that Moldovans are today in charge of their own destiny. This phenomenon in Moldova tallies with what sociologists say about social memory in general. Lyn Spillman, for example, theorizes about the longevity of social memory by noting that "there seems to be something more than institutionalized cultural production that gives collective memories long-term meaning."[15] Memories, she claims, are sustained in part by a "charisma of shared cross-generational narratives."[16] Sociologists Jeffery Olick and Joyce Robbins map out categories or "ideal types" of memory "persistence" or "change" to understand how and why memory

---

14 One informant used the term "occupied," and I use "occupation" because it best captures the consistent descriptions of Moldovans "submissive people" who are ruled by "regimes that come and go."

15 Lyn Spillman, "When Do Collective Memories Last? Founding Moments in the United States and Australia," in *States of Memory: Continuities, Conflicts, and Transformations in National Retrospection,* ed. Jeffrey K. Olick (Durham: Duke University Press, 2003), 167.

16 Ibid.

changes. They conclude that a particular memory either persists or changes for one of three types of reasons: instrumental, cultural, and inertial. An *instrumental* persistence or change is one that occurs intentionally; actors consciously try to affect the memory. A *cultural* persistence or change happens when people view the memory as still relevant or no longer important in daily life. Finally, an *inertial* persistence or change occurs unintentionally; a memory lives on "by sheer force of habit" or disappears because it is slowly forgotten.[17]

Memories of occupation persist in contemporary Moldovan society because of their cultural relevance and inertial persistence in everyday life. I had to look beyond the interview transcripts to understand this persistence. It was not enough to identify social memory in the interviews; I sought to understand why it still continued to have traction. The memories are strongest among those groups for whom "occupation" of one kind or another is still a daily reality. Put another way, while social memory cuts across all professional and social boundaries and runs parallel to the contemporary debates on what characterizes a Moldovan, social memory resonates more deeply with some Moldovans than with others, depending upon its relevance in everyday life. Teachers continue to work in hierarchical environments (e.g., top–down, school governance) that reinforce memories of occupation. For example, one teacher described that there is "no democracy" in her school because "whatever the director says is the law." She noted with some discouragement that "everything is being dictated from above." Teachers felt restricted by these structures and were also wary of directives from the Ministry of Education, which they viewed as more top-down decision-making in their lives.

Outside of school, teachers also felt constrained by society. Echoing the conversations about working in undemocratic spaces in their schools, discussions about the government, society, and "democracy" revealed that the teachers felt that they were not yet living in a democratic society. They felt that their

---

17 Olick and Robbins, "Social Memory Studies," 129.

government, from the local to national level, did not represent their interests but rather the interests of the "rich" or "business." Corruption has permeated all levels of Moldovan society from paying for grades in school to bribing ministry officials, and teachers often cited this as further proof that the government only works for some citizens — those who can afford to pay bribes.

On the surface, post-Soviet Moldova is dramatically different than its Soviet incarnation, centralized planning having given way to the free market and authoritarian rule having been supplanted by a democratic system. Many Moldovans, however, have yet to personally experience this transformation, and thus a social memory of "submission" remains salient in their everyday lives.

In Northern Ireland, teachers spoke about "getting on with it" or becoming "complacent" during The Troubles or how the conflict was "normalized" and a part of their everyday lives. Sharon, a grammar school teacher, recalled the conflict: "[i]t was just the way it was. I was probably only six or seven when it all started so I never knew any different. I suppose, from my teenage years in Belfast, shopping, and when you went through the security barriers, you were searched. […] And just when you're growing up, that's just what you knew. You didn't know any different and that was life and you just got on with it." My step is to investigate to the extent to which this memory manifests their lives today. Are they more accepting of collapsed government (at the time of this writing, The Northern Ireland Assembly has been non-functioning for over two years because of a disagreement of power-sharing between the two main political parties)? Do their memories of "getting on with it" insulate them from larger social and political forces that they cannot control? Or do these memories make them passive citizens? Questions like these underpin my next steps in my research as look deeply at teachers' lives outside their classrooms.

Discussion

Why Study Memory?

I never set out to study memory. In 2006, I competed my doctoral dissertation about history textbook reform and national identity in Moldova. I thought that I would move on to another project or area of the world. Yet, there were lingering puzzles in my data that I could not explain, and I left unexplored in my dissertation. My field notes and interview transcripts were littered with references to "patience," submission," and "peasants." For example, in 2004 I was having tea in the cramped office of the English language faculty at a local university. In discussing recent political events, a faculty member said that Moldovans were "too passive and too subdued" and then referenced the country's "Turkish domination" as a sort of an off-handed explanation (referring to the Ottoman Empire). I did not know how to make sense of these comments until I began to investigate them through the lens of social memory, which opened up a rich field of investigation into behavior and social change. For my work, it became a useful tool in understanding why teachers resisted education reforms, taught in certain ways, or made references to their students. It affirms that social memory is not just static thing, like a statue or museum, but a force that influences and shapes behavior.

The Moldovan case also demonstrates the importance of studying memory as practice, avoiding memory questions, and understanding social memory in the context of individuals' lives to reveal why memories persist. By examining memory practices, researchers can better understand which memories have value and importance in everyday life. One way to get at these practices is to ask individuals to talk about or tell stories about the past in general terms. The Moldovan case reveals that informants can consciously or unconsciously recall the expected past, such as describing the communist period as totalitarian or lacking in freedom. These discussions could easily confirm a researcher's preconceived ideas about a given society. But this social memory might not influence everyday behavior and attitudes. The more influential past and social memory — the one of submission and occupation in the Moldovan case — was much more amorphous. If we follow Halbwachs's theories of social memory, this unexpected social memory revealed much more about the present than the past. Moldovan teachers' memories about occupation surfaced in discussions about themselves rather than direct questioning about past regimes.

Researchers have to move beyond interview transcripts and the confines of interviews and discussions to understand social memory fully. These memories are embedded in the teachers' world, from the restrictions they feel in their work environment to the disconnection they feel from their government. By finding connections between the teachers' responses, their school environment, and their worlds outside the classroom, I could more accurately identify the teachers' social memory and understand why it is still relevant.

Who Are We When We Study Memory?

As I have discussed how certain words would trigger specific memories, a researchers' physical self — their presence — in an environment could also inform memories and narrative. Denzin reminds us that meaning is produced during the process of storytelling; narratives are "temporal productions" that are told and retold.[18] Likewise, the process of interpretation is just as fruitful. The researcher can never be removed from either the process, they can only try to interpret the narrative to the closest truth. Extending to social memory, the researcher's part in that process can vary depending on biography of that particular individual. In Moldova, I was frequently much younger than the teachers I interviewed, and they often treated me a junior colleague — they were often full of advice from professional suggestions to when I should get married and have children. My relative youth might have led some teachers to inhabit a less for-

---

18 Norman K. Denzin, *Interpretive Interactionism* (New York: Sage Publications, 2001).

mal or more familiar space during the time I spent with them, and this would have shaped their narrative.

This was apparent one afternoon in Alla's twelfth-grade history class. The lesson was not going as planned and her class was getting restless. She used me, the young researcher in the back of the room, as a diversion and asked me to tell the class about my impressions of Moldova. I told them that my first experience of Moldova was as a Peace Corps volunteer, and she asked about the Peace Corps. I explained that there were Peace Corps volunteers in Asia, in Africa, and all over the world. She asked if Moldova was like Africa. I told the class that Africa had different social problems, like HIV/AIDS, which blocked social and political development. Alla laughed at this and told the class, "If AIDS is Africa's block to development, then the government is our AIDS." Alla made this remark in a casual way and laughed some more. It revealed her feelings about the government, and in a very public way in front of her students — these feelings might not have come to light in a more formal setting.

In Northern Ireland, I am still uncovering the extent to which my American identity and presence as an American researcher shapes the process of storytelling and moving beyond the expected past. My interviews usually begin with a personal connection to the United States (one teacher spent summers pumping gas in New Jersey and another teacher's cousin lives in California or someone just returned from holiday in Florida). There are deep historical and cultural connections between the United States and Ireland and perhaps a shared social memory (e.g., migration). I often mention my great grandfather who emigrated from Donegal, who happened to be Protestant, but the fact that he was from a remote village in Donegal made this story appealing to teachers from both communities. To what extent are my subjects performing for me, an American? or an American with some Irish roots? Do we have a shared social memory? Unlike my work in Moldova, I have brought my husband and two young daughters with me to Northern Ireland. My older daughter once attended nursery school during an extended stay. This is often discussed; how might this further shape the stories that I hear? These questions will resonate throughout my continued fieldwork in Northern Ireland.

Lingering Questions

My ongoing work in Northern Ireland reveals that the unexpected past might be more difficult to tease out in some cases. Perhaps memory practices and everyday life in Northern Ireland will not be as closely aligned as in Moldova. What to make of Patrick and Frances? They were consciously performing the expected past for an outsider and yet they performed it anyway. It would be easy for a researcher to view these performances as confirmation of dominant narratives or stereotypes, but this might obscure other memories that are salient in their classrooms and everyday lives. Or what if the performance of the expected past inhibits individuals from developing their own narratives? How might this affect history teachers and their ability to interpret past events critically? Furthermore, to what extent do teachers need to perform specific memories for their students or other audiences? Almost all of Patrick's students were Catholic, and he noted that his students would most likely distrust a Protestant teacher. Do Patrick's performances of memory create and maintain trust in his classroom? Last, are Patrick's performances social memory? I return to the field with these lingering questions and with the aim of opening new avenues for understanding social memory practices in schools and beyond. Are you with me?

Bibliography

Ciscel, Matthew H. *The Language of the Moldovans: Romania, Russia, and Identity in an Ex-Soviet Republic*. Lanham: Lexington Books, 2007.

Denzin, Norman K. *Interpretive Interactionism*. New York: Sage Publications, 2001.

Halbwachs, Maurice. *On Collective Memory*. Chicago: University of Chicago Press, 1992.

Heintz, Monica, ed. *Weak State, Uncertain Citizenship: Moldova*. Frankfurt am Main: Peter Lang, 2008.

King, Charles. *The Moldovans: Romania, Russia, and the Politics of Culture*. Stanford: Hoover Institution Press, 2000.

Lather, Patti. "Critical Frames in Educational Research: Feminist and Post-structural Perspectives." *Theory into Practice* 31, no. 2 (1992): 87–99. DOI: 10.1080/00405849209543529.

Paxson, Margaret. *Solovyovo: The Story of Memory in a Russian Village*. Bloomington: Indiana University Press, 2005.

Olick, Jeffrey K., and Joyce Robbins. "Social Memory Studies: From 'Collective Memory' to the Historical Sociology of Mnemonic Practices." *Annual Review of Sociology* 24 (1998): 105–40. DOI: 10.1146/annurev.soc.24.1.105.

Spillman, Lyn. "When Do Collective Memories Last? Founding Moments in the United States and Australia." In *States of Memory: Continuities, Conflicts, and Transformations in National Retrospection,* edited by Jeffrey K. Olick, 161–92. Durham: Duke University Press, 2003.

Worden, Elizabeth Anderson. *National Identity and Educational Reform: Contested Classrooms*. New York: Routledge, 2014.

Young, James E. *The Texture of Memory: Holocaust Memorials and Meaning*. New Haven: Yale University Press, 1993.

Packing Up the Box of Tricks

Rosalie Metro & Felicitas Macgilchrist

As we reach the end of these pages, we have the urge to put away, to put to rest, to clean up, to give you something to take home. We pack the "questions" away first, and the last thing left will be the "ruins," which always undo our knowing anew. Whatever we have assembled in these chapters, we have left so much out. We have chosen, in this volume, not to discuss the classic differentiations among social, collective, connective, and public memory; nor have we entered the ongoing debate about whether memory is primarily individual or social or whether memory can ever be more than a metaphor when it is applied to socio-cultural practices. We have even resisted the temptation to reflect on how the concept of "memory" flags, in today's post-digital world, "a weird mixture of the ephemeral and the data trapped in physical media," which Colin Cummings's beautiful story on the limits of memory illustrates.[1] In the spirit of plural understandings, alternate pasts, and rhizomatic re-workings in the liminal space freed from these issues, we can make this ending just a pause for breath before sending you on your way.

---

1   Colin Cummings, "The Limits of Memory," *Third Space*, August 2018. Available at https://colincummings.ca/the-limits-of-memory.

1. QUESTIONS. (Elizabeth Anderson Worden) We can start with the questions we ask as researchers. In fact, we have to start there, with our responsibility for co-creating the past, for enabling people to remember and transforming memories into words in books like this one.

2. HISTORY. (Alexandra Oeser) When we look at the questions we ask, we can see that we have been constructing the discipline of memory studies in a hopeful attempt to free ourselves from the construction of the nation.

3. BODIES. (Rosalie Metro) We cannot evade others' suffering or our own. Counter-memory may not be a "solution" to the wrongs of history, but what else do we have?

4. RESPONSIBILITY. (Matthew Howard) Injustice exists, and we have the responsibility to remember it, particularly when this injustice is maintained in the failures of memory. The question is how and who and what structures are implicated in the process and performance of memory.

5. INNOCENCE. (Lisa Farley) We never were innocent — not when we were remembering the bravery of Australian war veterans nor when we are banning books that threaten to take away children's innocence.

6. MATERIALITY. (Alexandra Binnenkade & Felicitas Macgilchrist) While we may be guilty of misremembering or multiple remembering, the objects remain innocent in their materiality. They stubbornly persist or stubbornly disintegrate, regardless of our attachment to them.

7. RUINS. (Heidi Grunebaum) We find ourselves back among the ruins, at the start of our journey but transformed by it. The past stays but not the way we want it to. We cannot get rid of it, and we cannot get past it.

Are we still talking about memory? Are we ready to talk about power instead? Does the flurry of disarray in the trickbox generate ideas that take memory in new directions? This book ends with an invitation to look up from the trickbox, to look around at the expected and unexpected landmarks, the order and disorder, and to decide where in the assemblage you find yourself today.

Bibliography

Cummings, Colin. "The Limits of Memory." *Third Person,*
August 2018. Available at https://colincummings.ca/the-
limits-of-memory

www.ingramcontent.com/pod-product-compliance
Lightning Source LLC
Chambersburg PA
CBHW050652270326
41927CB00012B/2995